Tips and Traps When Building Your Home

Other McGraw-Hill Books by Robert Irwin

Tips and Traps When Building Your Home

Robert Irwin

McGraw-Hill

New York   San Francisco   Washington, D.C.   Auckland   Bogotá
Caracas   Lisbon   London   Madrid   Mexico City   Milan
Montreal   New Delhi   San Juan   Singapore
Sydney   Tokyo   Toronto

Library of Congress Cataloging-in-Publication Data

Irwin, Robert, 1941-
   Tips and traps when building your home / Robert Irwin.
     p.   cm.
   ISBN 0-07-135686-X
   1. House construction—Amateurs' manuals. 2. Building—Superintendence—Amateurs'
manuals. 3. Contractors—Selection and appointment—Amateurs' manuals. I. Title.

TH4815.178 2000
690'.837—dc21   00-039423

McGraw-Hill

A Division of The **McGraw·Hill** Companies

   8 9 0 FGR/FGR 0 9 8 7   690.8

                                   Irwin

ISBN 0-07-135686-X

Printed and bound by Quebecor World/Fairfield.

This publication is designed to provide accurate and authoritative information
in regard to the subject matter covered. It is sold with the understanding that
neither the author nor the publisher is engaged in rendering legal, account-
ing, or other professional service. If legal advice or other expert assistance is
required, the services of a competent professional person should be sought.
      —From a Declaration of Principles jointly adopted by a Committee
        of the American Bar Association and a Committee of Publishers.

Contents

CONSTRUCTION

THE AFTERMATH

Getting Started

1
Why Build It Yourself?

There are three reasons that most people build their own home. Can you find your reason among these?

- To design just what you want
- To save money
- To have the pleasure of doing it yourself

Let's consider them separately.

Can You Design Your Own Home?

Absolutely! After all, haven't you been living in homes all your life? Now's your chance to take all that practical living experience and winnow it down to what you really like and what you truly dislike. Then you get to put together a home that's built just the way you would like it to be.

Designing it yourself means you can choose how big (within your budget) the house will be, how the rooms will flow, what kind of rooms you will have (media room, great room, number of car spaces in garage, and so on), how much storage and where it will be located, which direction the house will present itself (front to the street, back to the view), and on and on.

Instead of having to accept what a builder thinks you want, you get to decide for yourself. Even on a strict budget, there are an enormous number of design decisions you can make. As a result, probably for the first time in your life, you'll end up with a house that truly fits you!

TRAP

There is a downside here you have to be careful of. Beware that if you build a home that is too specific to your needs, you might be creating a white elephant, a house that others (who likely will have different desires and needs) might not want to buy later on when you decide to sell. And rest assured, even though you believe you'll never sell the dream home you're constructing, you probably will. Statistics reveal that most people will sell after about 8 years. You need to balance your design with common sense.

Can You Save Money Building Your Own Home?

The answer here is a definite yes! While you can hire a contractor to do all the work, you can also do all or a part of it yourself. Just by being your own general contractor (and subcontracting out all the physical work) you can save anywhere from a low of around 15 percent to a high of 35 percent. The savings can go much higher if you do some of the actual physical work yourself.

Be sure you understand how significant this is. If your home costs $100,000 to build (not including the land), that's a savings of from $15,000 to $35,000 or more. That money may make the difference in your getting a lot in a better location (where you want to live, but otherwise can't afford to), or a bigger house, or a house with more quality finishing (better appliances, cabinets, carpets, and so forth). Or, of course, you could just pocket the savings! (On the first home I built, without lifting a hammer, my savings were 35 percent!)

What's involved is doing work that the general contractor (GC) normally does. Check Chapter 6 for details on that.

TIP

You have a better chance of getting exactly what you want if you act as your own GC. Most GCs have set ways of doing things and a few set plans they like to follow. Deviate from what they know or have previously done and they get nervous, tend to jack up the price, and fight you at almost every turn.

Will It Be Fun?

For this answer I can only tell you of my own experience and that of others. In a way, when you get two or more people together who have built their own homes, it sounds like a group of army buddies discussing war adventures.

Typically they will all have their own horror stories to recount, describing how the subcontractor put a roof on crooked, or how the plumber hooked the cold water line to the electrical service, or how the carpenters forgot to put on the diagonal bracing—and on and on. An observer might guess that these people had all shared terrible experiences.

Yet if you were to ask them if they would do it again, the vast majority would immediately say they'd jump at the chance. Indeed, most who have built their own homes say that the experience was one of the best of their lives. Yes, there were all sorts of things that went wrong—there always are. And most were caused by their own inexperience. But, overall, it was one of the most satisfying experiences they've ever had. In short, it was a ball, a ton of fun!

Have I sparked your interest? Chances are that if you've picked up this book, you're ready to move forward with building your own home. So let's get started. Here's how this book is organized. (Most authors never really explain their organization, so I thought this would be a good change of pace!)

In the next chapter we'll discuss designing the home. Then in the remainder of the first section, we'll talk about building an energy-efficient home, finding and evaluating the lot, finding a general contractor (or being one yourself and hiring subcontractors), getting a set of plans, getting bids and cost-cutting ideas, and arranging for financing.

My suggestion is that you read these chapters in the order in which they are presented. They should give you insights to help you avoid a host of pitfalls.

In the second part of the book we go into the actual construction. While this book is not designed to give you all the knowledge you need to physically build a home on your own from the ground up, it is designed to alert you to the traps along the way. And if you decide to do some of the work yourself, it will give you valuable tips on how to avoid smashed fingers and bad-looking results. (If you really want to physically build it from the ground up entirely on your own, there are a great number of books out there to help you. One of the best is Albert Dietz, *Dwelling House Construction,* 5th edition, MIT Press, Cambridge, Massachusetts, 1991.)

The last section is what happens after you build: taxation and selling (maybe!).

My own feeling is that before people die, one of the things that they should do in their life at least once is build their own home. This is your chance.

2
Designing Your Home

Do you want one story or two? What about a Cape Cod or a rambling ranch style? Do you want cathedral ceilings, view windows, or a big kitchen? What about the flow from room to room? How many bedrooms? Do you want a giant "great room," or would you rather have a separate dining room and family room?

These are just a few of the questions you get to answer when you design your own home. And answering them may be one of the most pleasurable experiences of your life. After all, most people never get the chance to design their own home. They buy ready-built by someone else and try to mold themselves to fit what's already there. You get the rare opportunity to design a home just to fit your tastes and desires!

Of course, along with choices come consequences. If it turns out you want a three-story circular home built over a marsh, you can pretty much forget about selling it later on. Build only what you like without a care for the rest of the world and you will create a financial disaster. Being practical about design means that you take into consideration what most people will accept and at least keep your design roughly within those bounds.

Nevertheless, you have enormous freedom when you design your own home, and you can build in all sorts of wonderful ways, within the bounds of common sense (as noted above) and, of course, your budget.

In this chapter we're going to look at some of the sources of inspiration you will want to use to help you plan your design.

TIP

Do your homework. Know what you want *before* you start building. You will save untold amounts of money by not changing your mind later on, necessitating ripping out and rebuilding.

Design Questions You Need to Answer

Here are some questions you need to answer when you consider the design of your new home:

1. Do you want your home to be formal or casual?

2. Do you prefer one story or two? (Two story is cheaper but sometimes inconvenient, particularly as you get older.)

3. Would you like three bedrooms or four? (Two are usually too few for later resale; five or more are costly, and this many means you'll have to resell mainly to large families.)

4. Do you want a great room (also called a "gathering room") which combines family, living, and dining rooms? It's in style now.

5. How many bathrooms do you want? (Two are minimal; three or four are considered more convenient and a plus when reselling.)

6. Where should the bathrooms go? (Obviously there will be one off the master bedroom, but what about the guest bathrooms? Keeping bathrooms in close proximity to each other saves money on plumbing, but may not place them where they are actually needed.)

7. Where should the laundry room go? (It's usually cheaper to have it near the garage or kitchen, but more convenient to have it near the bedrooms.)

8. Do you want a media room? (Nowadays this sometimes takes the place of a family room.)

9. Do you need a living room? (Most families rarely use it—sometimes a larger family room or media room will do.)

10. Do you want a warming/dressing room leading in from outdoors? (It's a plus in cold or hot climates.)

11. Where do you want the master bedroom to go? On the ground floor is more convenient. Away from the other bedrooms is nice in a family with kids. (In the back keeps street noise down.)

12. Do you want average or tall ceilings? (Tall ceilings add character but are inefficient for heating.)

13. Do you want a big kitchen with a large eating area in it? (If so, can you save money by skipping the formal dining room?)

14. How do you want the rooms to flow? (The dining room and family room should be near the kitchen; avoid long, dark hallways.)

15. How much storage space do you want? Where will it be located? (Many people use their garage for storage, but this usually means there isn't enough storage in the house proper.)

16. How do you want the presentation? (Should the house face the street? What if there's a view to the back?)

17. How many garage spaces—one, two, three, or more—do you want? (Remember, some people use the garage for storage, and so a larger garage is appreciated.)

These are just a few of the design questions you should address. Keep in mind that we haven't even gotten to the matter of finishing the home: What kind of fixtures, cabinets, floor covering, even paint colors do you want? We'll cover these in a later chapter.

Where Do You Get Answers?

There are a number of inexpensive resources available to you. Three of the best include:

1. New home designs (builders' model homes)

2. Magazines with floor plans of new homes

3. Computer design programs

From the moment you decide that you're going to build your own home (or even begin to suspect that this is something you want to do), you should be on the lookout for design answers. You will find them all over the place.

New Home Designs

You don't have to reinvent the wheel. Builders spend millions to come up with workable designs. Check them out.

And check out your friends' houses. You have friends that you visit. Now, when you go into their homes, look at the design with a critical eye. Look especially for features that you *don't* like. Begin making a list of the don'ts and dos. I like to keep a separate pad of paper for this by the side of my bed. I draw a rule down the center, and then at night before I go to sleep, I list any don'ts or dos that I've seen that day. If I wake up at night with what I think is a clever idea, I jot it down.

Also, make it a point to visit all the new homes in your area. The model homes are excellent teaching examples.

TIP

Keep in mind that all designs have common difficulties, such as dealing with hallways, rooms (or corners of rooms) without natural lighting, placement of doors and stairs, and so on. Try to see how builders succeed (or fail) in overcoming the inherent problems of design. After a while you'll begin to see certain patterns emerge that designers use over and over again.

Finally, if you're really thorough, you'll drive through neighborhoods looking for homes that are appealing from the outside. When you find one, check with an agent to see if there are any houses for sale that are of similar design and age located in the neighborhood. Sometimes, on a Sunday, houses for sale have an "open house," and if you stop by, you'll be able to walk in and see them. In other cases, a friendly real estate agent will be happy to take you by to see the inside.

By the way, you needn't use a subterfuge to get the agent to show you homes—you don't need to say you're really a buyer when you're not. Just explain that you're building your own home and that when you're done, you'll consider reselling. That's only the truth. An agent will be delighted to show you homes in the hopes of eventually getting a listing on yours—and possibly selling you another one.

Check Out Home Building Magazines

There are a host of magazines out there today that cater to home builders. Many are composed almost entirely of home design plans. You don't need to subscribe to or buy all of them (although you may want a subscription to one or two that you find particularly attuned to your needs). But you will find it helpful to obtain several issues of them.

Beware of home design magazines that just show a small, rough sketch of the house and then present full-page plans. Unless you are very adept at reading building plans, what you really need are photos or detailed sketches of both the exterior and interior to know what the home will actually look like. You may miss a detracting or an attractive feature when just seeing the plans.

In an ideal presentation, someone has already built the house, and thus there are photos of it from multiple angles. This lets you get a sense of what it really looks like.

TRAP

Keep in mind that in some cases, the plans found in magazines are nothing more than the concept of some architect or draftsperson. Maybe they will make sense in the real world, and maybe not. For that reason, once you find a plan you really like, it's always a good idea to take it to an architect or draftsperson to have it evaluated and adapted to your specific needs. Many architects will do an evaluation for a moderate fee.

If you do find a plan that seems to suit you well, you can usually get a full set of building plans from the publication for around $500. Typically there is a sliding scale based on how many copies you buy. For example, for the first set the cost might be $400. For four full sets it might be $500. For ten sets it could be $600, and so forth.

Keep in mind that you will need at least three or four sets: one for yourself, one for the master builder or subcontractor(s) you hire (unless you do the work yourself), and one for the building department when you get permits. You may also need additional sets if you want a lumber supply house to do a "takeoff"—an estimate of the cost for all the supplies you need. On the other hand, if you're going to have an architect change the plans to meet your needs, you'll only need one set from the magazine company.

TIP

For a few dollars more, most of the magazines will also supply a specifications (spec) sheet detailing all the materials you'll need, often down to the nails and screws required. Be sure to get this, as it's invaluable when estimating costs and procuring building supplies.

MAGAZINES TO CHECK OUT

Home. A great place to find the fixtures you will need. It also shows how to use space effectively.

Home and Architectural Trends. Clues you in on the latest developments in design. Be aware, however, that you'll need a fat pocketbook to use them.

Homestyles Home Plans. Gives you layouts, plans, and sketches. You can purchase blueprints and specs for a fee.

Taunton's Fine Home Building. Explains the latest building techniques. Gives some excellent specifics.

This Old House. From the TV shows—covers all aspects of building and landscaping.

Some home design magazines are widely sold as special single issues or annual issues. Check on the newsstands for publications with elevations and plans in them. There are often dozens available.

Check Out Computer Programs

A number of programs are available that will run on most home computers that can aid you in designing your home. These programs will allow you to generate a three-dimensional presentation of your home and let you play "what-if" games with it.

For example, you can move the rooms around. What if the family room were in front instead of the back? Or what if the kitchen were smaller and the media room larger? And so on. With just a few key and mouse clicks, you can see how the change will look.

These programs are relatively inexpensive, given the overall cost of building a home, and can be worth your while. Further, many of them will generate building plans, sometimes in great detail. (I would certainly want to have these plans evaluated by an architect!)

On the downside, the learning curve on all the programs I've tried has been rather steep. Plan on spending some time figuring out just how they work. Some of the better programs include:

Sierra Home Architect 2.0 (or higher). Lets you actually design your home and offers photo-realistic three-dimensional plans you can "walk through."

3D Home Architect 3.0 (or higher) (by Broderbund). Allows you to design your home from the ground up.

What About Hiring an Architect?

It really depends on how thick your wallet is. An architect is the professional whose job it is to come up with home designs. Hire an architect and you've got a pro working for you.

This is how they typically operate: First of all, they will want some sort of up-front fee to ensure that you are really serious about doing the work. Then, they will talk with you, and show you design ideas in books and magazines as well as plans and sketches of their earlier projects. When they have a good idea of what you want, they'll usually make sketches called "elevations," typically exterior but perhaps with a few inside views. You can see how the home will look and then make adjustments or changes. When everything is just as you like, they'll draw up a set of plans that any competent builder can follow.

How much will all this cost you? It depends on the deal you strike. Typically an architect will want a percentage of the overall construction costs, anywhere from 3 to 15 percent, depending on the reputation of the architect as well as how much work is done. (Elevations or sketches, for example, give you the clearest view of what the home will look like, but they can take a long time to create.)

TRAP

In some cases an architect will work on an hourly basis. While at first this may seem like a cost cutter, just be sure the total doesn't come out to more than a percentage would have cost you.

While the cost of an architect is high, the results are usually worth it. Often architects can anticipate problems with the lay of the land or with a particular design feature that you were blind to. They can point these problems out and then make changes in the plans, thus saving you thousands of dollars later on in the construction phase.

TIP

If you know exactly what you want, you may not need the services of a full architect. Rather, a draftsperson may do. This is someone who has drafting skills and can execute a set of plans, provided you come up with all the specifics. Draftspeople are available under the heading "Drafting" in the yellow pages. Their fees are usually a fraction of what an architect charges. (But, then again, they only provide a limited service.)

Avoid Basic Flaws When Designing Your Home

There are a series of design flaws that tend to crop up whenever you are constructing a home. It's simply in the nature of getting all the rooms you want into the compact area of a home. Here are the big 10 to watch out for:

10 DESIGN FLAWS TO AVOID

1. Long hallways (waste of space)
2. Inappropriate connecting rooms (such as a bathroom off the kitchen)
3. Dark corners in big rooms such as the living room

4. Awkward layout (bad walking flow from room to room)

5. Master bedroom in front (where most street noise is)

6. Stairways directly behind front door (leads you upstairs instead of into the family areas downstairs)

7. Back door directly past the front door through one or two open rooms (see out the back from the front—makes the house feel small and inadequate)

8. Walk-through rooms (can only get to the guest bathroom by walking through a bedroom)

9. Small windows (don't let in enough light or air)

10. Square or boxy look that's dull and boring

The above flaws crop up whenever home design is involved. It's how they are solved that makes for a beautiful home.

Typical Design Problem— The Kitchen

To help you design your kitchen, here are some questions you will want to answer:

KITCHEN QUESTIONNAIRE

1. Do you regularly prepare meals in your kitchen rather than eat out?   Yes [   ] No [   ]

   If you prepare meals, you'll want a kitchen that has lots of countertop space. If you usually just bring in meals, you'll want more room for a table where you can sit and eat.

2. How many people in the family are cooks?

   One [   ] Two [   ] Three [   ]

   If only one person cooks, then you need a relatively small work area. But if several people cook simultaneously, you'll want separate cooking stations.

3. How many people regularly eat in the kitchen? _____

   You may have a large family, but they may not all eat together. In that case a countertop table with high chairs may be useful. If you all eat together on a regular basis, however, you may want room for a large table and chairs.

4. How much food do you buy at once?   A lot [   ] A little [   ]

Some people go out and buy their food for preparation each day. Others buy in bulk and store it. If you plan on storing a lot of food, you'll want extra cabinets and storage space.

5. Will you have children in your kitchen?   Yes [   ] No [   ]

If so, cabinets that lock may be a good idea. (As well, some stoves do not have lock-outs that would safety-proof them.) You'll also want to consider an outlet for a TV. Perhaps an area for games would be appropriate. What about a surface to accommodate a computer?

6. Do you use your kitchen as a meeting place?   Yes [   ] No [   ]
Do you read or study in the kitchen?   Yes [   ] No [   ]

For some families, the kitchen is the main room of the house. If that's the case, you'll want as large a kitchen as possible with lots of space for chairs and tables. Perhaps the countertop area will be at a minimum. Also, you may want to increase the amount of lighting or direct it over certain areas.

7. What appliances do you want in the kitchen? _____

You will certainly want a stove, oven, and sink. What about a garbage disposal and dishwasher, considered necessary in most kitchens? What about a trash compactor, towel warmer, instant hot water delivery system, built-in microwave? What about built-in countertop items such as a blender and can opener? It's a good idea to make a list of all the items you want in the kitchen so you'll be sure to leave space for them.

8. Are you thinking in terms of a workstation triangle?

Yes [   ] No [   ]

Placing frequently used items in groups of three works well. For example, having the stove, oven, and microwave together is a food preparation triangle. Having the sink, dishwasher, and countertop space together makes for a cleanup triangle.

9. Have you considered the traffic flow?   Yes [   ] No [   ]

Now is the chance to set it up. Make sure you can easily get from one side of the kitchen to the other. Also, be sure the doors are logically placed.

10. Have you considered safety and efficiency issues?

Yes [   ] No [   ]

You won't want an oven door that opens into a walk area. You won't want a dishwasher door so close to the sink that it bangs your knees when you try to use it.

11. Have you created a "wants list" and prioritized it?

Yes [   ] No [   ]

The fact is you probably won't be able to get everything you want in your kitchen because of space or budgetary concerns. So what must you have, and what can you do without?

Typical Design Problem— The Bathroom

To help you design your bathroom, here are some questions you'll want to answer:

BATHROOM QUESTIONNAIRE

1. Will there be two people using the bathroom simultaneously?

Yes [   ] No [   ]

If so, you'll need to install two sinks instead of one. As a general rule in the modern house, two sinks in a master bedroom are considered the norm. One in the main bathroom or guest bathroom is still all right.

2. How many bathrooms do you need in the house? _____

These days, two bathrooms are considered minimal. In most moderate to upscale houses, at least three (master, main, and guest) are considered desirable. More than three will enhance the house, but will probably not return much money on the dollar in terms of an investment. Also, expanding families, particularly as children become teenagers, increase the need for an additional bathroom.

3. Do you need lots of countertop space? Yes [   ] No [   ]

You may discover that what you really want in a bathroom is space for combs, brushes, hair driers, and so on. Now's the time to add it in.

4. Do you want a shower, a tub, or a tub shower? _____

It depends on what you like. Some people prefer showers exclusively, others baths, and still others a combination. Ideally, the shower will be separate from the tub at least in the master bedroom. There's a safety concern here—a separate shower is easier to get into and out of than a tub used as a shower combo since the floor surface in the shower is usually less slick than the tub's bottom.

5. Do you want storage in the bathroom?   Yes [   ] No [   ]

    You'll need to have space to store toilet paper and other toiletries. What about towels and linen? And then there are cleaning detergents as well as medications and first-aid items. While you may not need much space, each family is different. You may want to consider additional cabinets.

6. Will you want extra lighting?   Yes [   ] No [   ]

    These days most building departments usually insist that there be at least one fluorescent light in a bathroom to give adequate lighting. However, that may simply not be enough, the light may not be where you want it, or you may not like the cool light produced. You may want to add additional directed spot or wall incandescent lights. Not only do these make the room brighter, but their yellow cast makes it warmer.

7. Will you buy water-saving fixtures?   Yes [   ] No [   ]

    In many parts of the country, water is scarce and getting scarcer. When installing toilets, faucets, and shower heads, you will want to be sure they restrict the flow of water.

Designing My Home

At the same time as I am writing this book, my wife and I are in the design phase of the next home we will build. An example of some of the design choices we've made may be helpful in letting you see how such decisions come about. Keep in mind that your choices may be far different. You'll need to make these or similar choices on your own.

MY DESIGN CHOICES

1. Single story, 2500 square feet, three-car garage. (These days the minimum size for a resalable home in most areas is 2000 feet.)

2. Small, formal dining room. (While no longer a necessity, it's great for entertaining small groups.)

3. Great room (incorporating both the traditional family room and living room—my feeling is that most people just don't use a living room anymore.)

4. Large kitchen with small eating area. (For when just the family is at home.)

5. Small dressing room (with a sink) off the kitchen, leading out to the backyard.

6. Media room incorporating computer, TV, audio, and gaming. (This has become a necessity in our Internet world.)

7. Three large bedrooms (one master, one guest, and one doubling as an office), with large closets in each.

8. Three large bathrooms (one off the master bedroom, one between the two other bedrooms, and one guest bathroom near the great room).

9. Laundry room off the master bedroom (the most convenient location).

10. Master bedroom, kitchen, and great room at the rear of the home; dining room, guest bedrooms, and office toward the front. Entrance hall into the great room. (This helps traffic flow and reduces street noise in the rooms occupied in the evening and night.)

11. Cathedral ceilings in the great room and master bedroom only. Conventional ceilings elsewhere.

12. Presentation to the back, where there is a view.

13. Large windows toward the back.

3
Building an Energy-Efficient Home

I can still remember my grandfather telling me stories of the cold winters he spent in the Northwest. One of his pet peeves involved the old pot-bellied stoves used for heating. He said the family would gather round the heater on the coldest winter nights to keep warm. The front of their bodies would be sweating from the heat radiated by the stove. Yet their backs would be freezing from the cold air in the room. It was impossible to get warm all over.

Modern homes don't, or shouldn't, have such problems. Today it's possible through the judicious use of insulating materials and heating and air conditioning systems to have a home that is consistently warm in winter and cool in summer. And all this can be accomplished while keeping energy costs low.

However, not all insulating/heating/cooling plans work as well as others. Making some prudent choices during the design stage of the home can add or markedly detract from the home's energy efficiency.

Where Thermal Transmission Occurs

Heat transfer (either loss of heat from the inside to the outside during winter or the opposite during summer) occurs at all exterior surfaces of the home. However, the heat transfer occurs at different rates for different areas.

Ceilings

Since heat rises, one of the biggest sources of heat transfer is through the ceiling. An uninsulated attic will mean that during winter, heat in the home will quickly rise, move through the ceiling into the attic space, and then escape through the roof. Thus, even in mild climates where temperatures rarely dip below 40 degrees Fahrenheit, the home will still be uncomfortably cold in winter.

Similarly, during the summer, the sun burning down on the roof will raise the attic temperature. Sometimes attics can get as hot as 140 to 160 degrees on hot summer days. The heat from the attic will work its way down into the living area below very quickly, making it uncomfortable to be in the house.

Thus, insulating the attic to avoid this heat transfer is a must-do.

Walls and Windows

Just as heat is transferred through the ceiling, it is also transferred through the exterior walls and windows. The heat transfer through single-pane window glass, however, is far greater than through uninsulated walls. This problem often gets overlooked because there is so much more wall area in the home than window area. As a result, many people tend to overlook windows and be more concerned with wall insulation. However, in the average home as much heat is transferred through the glass as through all the walls! That means that as much attention must be paid to window energy conservation as to wall insulation.

Foundation, Floors, and Basement

Since we all know that heat rises, it is a surprise to many people to learn that there is significant heat transfer through the foundation, floors, and basement. Yet this phenomenon is readily observable in a poorly insulated home. Regardless of the heating system, here you will quickly become aware of cold spots on the floor near the exterior walls.

Thus insulating the foundation, floors, and basement (if you have one) is also a excellent idea, particularly in areas of severe temperatures.

Doors and Openings

Air transfer through doors that don't fit tightly as well as through air gaps inside walls and near ceilings (these occur during construction) can significantly add to the heat transfer of the home. Therefore, weather stripping of doors is a must, and sealing of all air gaps during framing is likewise important.

How Is a Home Insulated?

A wide variety of materials can be used to insulate a home. These materials are given an "R-rating," which is essentially their resistance to heat transfer. There are two important things to remember about R-values: The first is that every type of material has a different value. The second is that the R-value always increases with the increased thickness of the material. Here are some relative R-values for different types of commonly used insulation and building materials:

COMPARING APPROXIMATE R-VALUES

Material	Thickness		
	1 inch	4 inches	6 inches
Bricks	.2	.8	1.2
Concrete (poured)	.08	.32	.5
Fiberglass	3	11	19
Glass	.9	n/a	n/a
Paper (celullose fiber)	3.5	14	22
Plywood (5/8 inch)	1.25	n/a	n/a
Polystyrene (rigid boards)	4.6	22	28
Rockwool (batts)	3.5	14	22
Rockwool (blown)	3	11	19
Vermicullite	2	8	19

TRAP

One of the problems in construction is getting a high enough R-value given the space allowed. For example, in a home built with 2 × 4-inch studs, the available space in the walls for insulation is only 3.6 inches. Thus, if you use fiberglass blankets, the highest R-value you can approximate is R-ll. On the other hand, if you use 2 × 6 studs in the exterior walls, you have roughly 5.5 inches available and can approach R-19. For this and other reasons, homes built in severe climates should have thicker walls.

TIP

You can increase the insulating value by changing the type of insulation. For example, rigid boards of polystyrene will give much higher R-values than blankets of fiberglass. However, the trade-off comes in cost. The rigid boards cost significantly more.

Insulating Windows

Since there is so much heat transfer through glass, one of the primary concerns when designing the home is to get better R-values here. As a result, today most building departments, even in areas of moderate climate, insist that you use double-pane glass. Simply by using two panes instead of one, you double the R-value from roughly 1 to 2. While that may not seem like such a significant increase, it in effect cuts the heat loss through the glass in half.

The two panes have a dead-air space in between that is hermetically sealed. Adding an inert gas, such as argon, also can increase the R-value. Inert gasses are heavier than air, meaning that their molecules move slower, thus reducing conductivity.

TRAP

In the past it was often the case that home builders wishing to increase the insulating properties of windows would use triple-pane glass (achieving roughly R-3). I don't recommend this, as my experience with triple-pane windows is that they can sometimes be heavy and awkward to open and close and that the significantly higher cost is not justified.

Low-Emissivity Glass

A new alternative is low-E (low-emissivity, high-transmittance) glass. Low-E glass is glass that has been coated with a material that reduces heat conductivity. At the same time, almost all natural light is still able to come through.

Low-E glass is high tech and produces some amazing results. While a single pane of glass, as noted, is roughly R-1, low-E glass can have an R-value of anywhere from 4 to as much as 7 or more. Further, because there is just a coating, it doesn't much affect the weight of the glass. That means that the windows are easy to open and close.

The downside is that, as of this writing, low-E glass coating is expensive. Nevertheless, you can often make up the cost of the coating in just a few years of energy savings.

Insulating Ceilings

As noted above, probably the greatest single area of heat transfer is through the ceiling and roof. Therefore, the logical place to put insulation is in the attic. The general rule is that the more insulation here, the better.

TIP

The building department will usually specify the R-rating for insulation in your area. For example, in temperate climates it may indicate R-19 for ceilings. In severe climates it may jump that up to R-32 or higher. However, these are minimums. You may want to exceed these ratings to give your home more insulating qualities.

Usually insulation in the form of fiberglass blankets or batts (a batt is simply a slightly more rigid section of a blanket anywhere from 4 to 8 feet long) is placed in the attic between the studs directly above drywall. This forms a thermal barrier that prevents heat transmission.

TIP

Insulating only the ceiling causes the attic to become a heat trap in the summer. As noted earlier, attic temperatures can get excessive. The result is that in the evening when temperatures cool down outside, the hot attic continues to transfer heat downward into the house and prevents the home from quickly cooling off. Installing several attic fans (with automatic controls to turn them on as the temperature rises) will cool the attic in summer and avoid the problem of slow cooldown.

Insulating Walls

While it is commonly assumed that the only insulation one need be concerned with in walls is the fiberglass blankets typically rolled up into them, that's actually not the case. The wood blocks placed in walls as firebreaks also perform an insulating function. They prevent air movement up from the bottom of the airspace to the top and the resultant heat transfer. Therefore, care should be taken that they are in place in all exterior walls.

It is also important that there be no gaps at the top of the wall where it joins the attic space. Usually a top plate will terminate the wall, and the ceiling rafters will go above that, eliminating the problem–but not always, depending on the construction used.

TIP

It's a good idea when the framing is completed, but before the wallboard is installed, to check along the top of the walls where they join the ceiling rafters to see if there are any openings connecting the wall airspace to the attic airspace where air can move. If there are, solid blocking (wood blocks) can be used to close the openings and prevent air movement. If the openings are relatively small, expansive foam (available in convenient cans) may be used to fill them. This same remedy can also be used in cases where vents, wiring, and ductwork have left small gaps or openings.

Insulating Foundations, Basements, and Slabs

In order to prevent cold spots near the bottom of exterior walls and at the exterior edges of floors of the home in cold climates, insulation should be placed on the exterior of the foundation as well as beneath any concrete slabs. Additionally a moisture barrier (impermeable membrane) should be placed immediately beneath the slab and facing inward behind any insulation on the foundation or basement walls (see below).

Also, it's usually a good idea to use a sill sealer, a thin layer of insulation between the concrete foundation and the wood sill that goes on top of it. This prevents air from moving through uneven spaces at the top of the cement foundation.

Moisture Barriers

Not long ago I was talking with a person from the Midwest who had a perplexing moisture problem in her home. She was living in an apartment that was partly below ground level. While the living area was well insulated, in the winter whenever she turned on the heat, thick moisture would form on the windows and the exterior walls. Nothing she could do seemed to alleviate the problem. The solution to her dilemma only came about when she removed the inside wallboard and installed a vapor barrier immediately behind it.

While insulating a home may seem straightforward—you simply put insulating materials everywhere possible—actually the matter is complicated by the element of moisture. From a basic physics point of view, warm air can hold far more moisture than cool air. That's the reason that early air conditioners produced so much moisture that they were impractical in homes. By cooling the air, moisture was forced out of it. It condensed and hung in droplets everywhere. It wasn't until manufacturers learned to combine a dehumidifier with a cooling unit that modern air conditioning became practical.

In terms of a home, the air temperature at the surface of the inside exterior wall may be 70 degrees, while the temperature at the surface of the outside exterior wall may be 30 degrees (or much lower in areas of severe cold). While insulation allows us to have such great differentials and to keep our house warm, most insulating materials do little to prevent moist air from passing through. Thus moist air passing from the inside of the home to the exterior wall experiences a severe temperature drop. Since the colder air cannot support as much moisture, condensation occurs.

The point at which condensation occurs is called the "dew point." If it occurs inside the wall, the inside wall will "sweat" and eventually produce mildew and rot. Sometimes, however, particularly if the insulation is not sufficient to reduce heat loss and the inside of the interior wall gets cold, sweating can actually occur on the interior drywall surface. When inside and touching a wall with this problem, the wall will feel cold *and* wet. Moisture on such surfaces, besides being unpleasant to live with, may cause mold, mildew, and destruction of walls, furniture, and even apparel.

The problem is alleviated by installing sufficient insulation to keep the inside of the exterior wall warm. Additionally, if a vapor barrier is placed immediately behind the drywall, moist air will not be able to pass through. That's the reason that most blanket as well as batt insulation comes with a vapor barrier (often tarred paper or impermeable plastic) glued to one side. When the insulation is nailed to the studs with the vapor barrier to the inside, it prevents moist air from traveling through the wall where, as the temperature drops, it will reach the dew point and produce unwanted condensation. (Figure 3-1.)

Vapor barriers should be placed in the walls, in the roof, in the foundation, in the bottom floor, and around the basement, *always facing inward.*

TIP

While builders will almost always install blanket insulation correctly on ceilings and walls, they will sometimes install it incorrectly on floors—with the vapor barrier

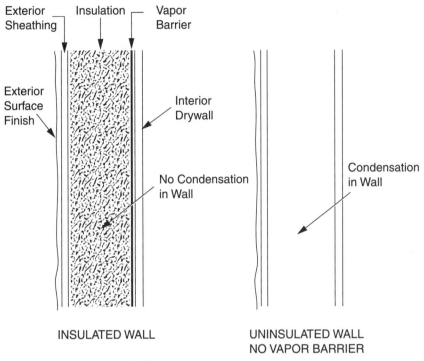

Figure 3-1. Moisture in Wall

pointing down (away from the floor). For floors, the insulation should be installed with the vapor barrier up. The insulation is then supported by wires hung between the joists.

When installing a vapor barrier in a foundation or basement, it should be placed immediately below the slab and on the exterior of the basement walls or the foundation. (Figure 3-2.)

Heating Systems

One of the big choices you will have when building your own home is the type of heating system to use. A variety of systems are available, each with its own pluses and minuses. Your choice should reflect the type of weather conditions in your locale as well as the ratio of the cost of the system to its efficiency.

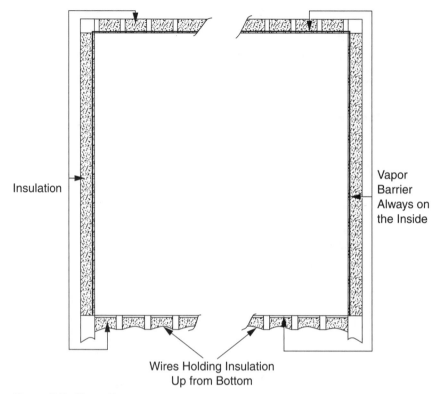

Insulation

Vapor
Barrier
Always on
the Inside

Wires Holding Insulation
Up from Bottom

Figure 3-2. Vapor Barrier

Energy used to fuel a heating system can come from a variety of sources.

ENERGY SOURCES

Coal. Inexpensive, yet infrequently used today primarily because of its production of toxic by-products released into the atmosphere. Must be vented.

Electricity, Offers the cheapest installation and appliance cost. However, in most areas it is the most costly to operate. No venting required. The cleanest of the various fuels.

Gas (natural or propane). A relatively cheap source of fuel in most areas. However, good gas furnaces can be expensive and must be vented. Considered a clean fuel since most of it is consumed during burning.

Oil (fuel). Relatively inexpensive. However, requires frequent "tuning" of fuel oil heating unit for maximum efficiency and is expensive to install because it requires a storage tank, usually underground. Must be vented. Moderately clean.

Solar. Expensive installation. Efficiency depends on the amount of sunlight available. More popular a few years ago than now. Does not require venting and is a clean source of energy.

Wood. Stoves that burn wood or pellets (compressed wood) are fairly expensive because of increasingly strict environmental rules. In some areas certain types are outlawed, so be sure to check. Having to haul and store wood is a definite drawback. Wood burns dirty even in the best of wood-burning stoves. Must be vented.

What Type of Delivery System Works Best?

There are basically just two types of delivery systems for heat. What I call the "convection" system is the typical blower furnace. There are ducts leading from the furnace to the various rooms in the house and a return bringing home air back to the furnace. In a properly operated blower system, at no time does the air from the house mix with the air in the combustion chamber. Rather, the home air is run across the surface of a metal "heat exchanger." Home air is on one side, and air from combustion is on the other— they never mix.

TRAP

To reduce costs, in most forced-air systems the ducts are in the ceiling or are located high on the walls. (The vents can be run cheaply through the attic.) Because of their height, this makes for good air conditioning but poor heating. Hot air rises, so when heating from high ducts, the lower portion of the room never really gets fully warmed. While the top portion of the room may be 72 degrees, the lower portion (around your feet) can be 10 to 15 degrees cooler. Ideally, separate high ducts would be used for air and low ducts for heating, although this is almost never done because of cost.

The forced-air furnace works with many different types of fuels and is probably the most commonly used heating system in homes. Since it already incorporates a blower and ducts, it is relatively easy to install an air conditioning and humidifying system to it. However, it has important drawbacks that should be considered.

BLOWER FURNACE PROS AND CONS

Pluses

- An entire home can be heated up in a matter of minutes. The reason is that the air is basically exchanged, hot air replacing cold.
- The same ducts that supply hot air can be used to supply the cold air of an air conditioning unit.
- It's easy to connect a humidifier to the system.
- Filters are a normal part of the system, and so the air is cleaned as it circulates.
- A variety of fuels including gas, oil, coal, and wood can be used to run it. Solar and electrical installations are less common.

Minuses

- The temperature in the home does not remain constant. When it drops, the furnace goes on blowing hot air until the temperature rises. Then it shuts off until the temperature falls. Thus the furnace is constantly cycling on and off, and the temperature in the home goes up and down at a minimum 3 to 4 degrees.
- Unless a heavy-duty filtration system is installed and constantly maintained, the system blows minute particles around the home, making it uncomfortable for those with breathing problems. It can also spread viruses and bacteria.
- The furnace can be noisy. In older systems with metal ducts, the expansion and contraction of these ducts as they heat and cool can also be noisy. In modern systems with solid fiberglass ducts, it's less of a problem.

- It is difficult to have true zone heating. While a register in a particular room may be closed, most of the registers must remain open in order for the system to get enough air flow to operate properly. In some homes a flap in a duct may be opened or closed to allow hot air to move to one section of a house or another, but again enough registers must be open for the system to have sufficient air to operate.

- Hot air tends to dry out the home; thus a humidifier is recommended, particularly in dry parts of the country.

TIP

Traditionally, ducts for blower furnaces have been made out of sheet metal. Newer ducts, however, are formed out of solid fiberglass insulation. They provide air transport and at the same time insulate the hot air. Also, they are extremely quick and easy to install.

Radiant Heating

The other type of system commonly used is radiant heating. Here a radiator, metal stove, or even ceramic glass is heated, and it radiates heat into the room. Rather than the air being exchanged and warmed, as in a blower furnace system, the objects in the room are warmed. Radiant systems are among both the oldest and most modern methods of heating homes. As highly efficient radiant systems have been developed over the last few years, they have increased in popularity.

One of the most commonly used radiant heating systems involves a boiler for heating water and a copper tubing circulating system that distributes the heated water to baseboard or other types of radiators in every room of the home. Since the radiators in each room can be opened or closed, as well as different temperatures set for different areas of the house (such as different floors of the home), this system offers true zonal heating. Air filtration, cooling, and humidifying/dehumidifying, however, must be added separately.

Wood-burning stoves are another source of radiant heat. But since they are located in a single spot, they don't supply heat evenly throughout a home. They can however, heat very large areas quite efficiently. (It is possible to connect a water distribution system to a wood-burning stove, although the results I've seen have been less than satisfactory, often having leaks.)

A better choice, in my opinion, is a gas heater (fueled by either natural gas or propane). In direct-vent models, air from the outside is drawn in (as part of the venting system) and used for combustion, then vented out. The air from the home never gets used up to operate the heater (an important consideration when these units are placed in small areas such as bedrooms).

Gas heaters are available in a wide variety of designs, from ultra-modern to traditional (where they look like the old wood-burning stoves of the last century). Many offer large glass fronts with ceramic logs and flames. Most of these units are airtight. For those that are, none of the products of combustion get into the home, and so they may be used in small areas such as bedrooms.

TIP

My personal choice for heating is radiant. While it takes longer to heat up a home, once the home is heated, the temperature remains constant. Also the energy costs are usually lower.

Newer ventless models have also been introduced. Their primary advantage is that they don't require venting. However, they do use up air from the home and have not been approved for use in every state. I have qualms about using them in a small, confined area such as a bedroom.

RADIANT HEATER PROS AND CONS

Pluses

- Very clean heat. An excellent source of heating for those with breathing problems.
- True zonal heating. You get the heat just where you want it. Also, different zones can have different temperatures.
- Even heat. The temperature variations take place slowly, and hence are not usually noticeable.

- Generally silent, although systems employing heavy metal heaters will give off creaks and groans as they expand and contract.

Minuses

- A humidifier or air cleaner cannot be included in the system. Rather, they must be added separately at an additional cost.
- The units themselves and the distribution systems tend to be costly and can sometimes be expensive to install. (Electrical systems are relatively cheap to install; hot water systems, on the other hand, are expensive to install.)
- They are slow. It takes a long time to heat a house. Going from 35 degrees to 70 degrees can take many hours.
- The systems tend to dry out the air, so a humidifier is almost a necessity in all but the wettest climates.
- Radiator surfaces (as in electrical or gas stove radiators) can get very hot, posing a threat, especially to children, of getting burned.

TRAP

The least expensive system to buy and install when constructing your home is electrical. However, if you do so, you will probably be penny-wise and pound-foolish. Electrical is the most expensive to operate (and sometimes the least efficient in heating) in most areas.

What About Fireplaces?

In a nutshell, there's no place for an open fireplace in a modern home. Open fireplaces are the most inefficient of heating systems. They were developed in the Middle Ages and used to heat castles by people who simply didn't know any better. Their usage has continued until current times, today more for sentimental than other reasons. Most people just love the romantic idea of sitting by an open fire, and freezing.

If you think about it, the problem with an open fireplace quickly becomes apparent. Burning logs heat air, which rises quickly to escape out the chimney. But where does the air that's heated come from? It has to come from the house. As soon as air from the house is sucked into the fireplace, cold air from outside is sucked into the house to replace it. Thus, a fireplace actually cools rather than heats a home. (Of course, there is some radiant heat which does warm the area immediately adjacent to the fireplace.)

If you want the appearance of an open fire, but also want an efficient room heating device, there are alternatives. A closed fireplace is one. Here a glass and metal screen covers the entire fireplace opening, creating a seal. You can regulate the amount of air going in, thus cutting down on the amount of cold air being sucked into the home. And the glass itself radiates some heat outward. It's not as efficient as other solutions, but it's far better than an open fireplace.

The drawback with a glass screen is that it can be expensive if it's made right with ceramic glass. Inexpensive glass screens usually can't take the heat of a big fire. Further, every time you open the glass doors to put in a log, the fireplace sucks cold air into the house.

Some fireplaces have heat exchangers and fans built into them. The heat exchanger is usually a large piece of metal located in the back wall of the fireplace. A blower and vents direct air across the exchanger, which heats the air. Then the air is blown into the room. This is a yet more efficient fireplace.

Perhaps the best solution, as noted earlier, is to install a gas heater (appliance) with ceramic logs. Gas heaters can give the appearance of a fireplace, except that they have a permanently sealed heavy ceramic glass plate in front. The glass gets very hot and radiates heat. Behind the glass, ceramic logs can have flames dancing on them, so the similarity to a wood-burning fireplace is striking.

The gas heater, while expensive, is usually far less expensive than building a masonry chimney for an open fireplace. And, of course, there's no messing with logs. Best of all, when you want to light it, you simply flip a switch!

TRAP

Because of the polluting effects of burning wood, many areas are increasingly banning the installation of wood-burning fireplaces. You may not have a choice of having one in your area.

4

Finding the Land

The single biggest mistake that people make when building a home is to scrimp on the land.

Saving money on land is always possible. Whether you're buying in a city development or out in a rural area, there will always be some lots that appear to be bargains, that cost much less than surrounding lots. You'll be thinking to yourself that if you can save $10,000, $20,000, or even $50,000 on the lot, that's just more money you can put into the house.

This is another case where it doesn't pay to be penny-wise and pound-foolish: A lot that is priced too low almost always has a problem that you don't want to buy into. On the other hand, a lot that is high-priced often has advantages that will add to your enjoyment while you own it and bring in top dollar when you sell.

TIP

Always buy the best lot you can afford.

Here's a test. In a nearby area with a lake and a golf course, three types of lots are available. The highest-priced lots are right on the water and cost around $200,000 each. The mid-priced lots have a view of the water (but are not on it) or are next to a golf course and cost around $100,000. The least expensive lots have neither water, view, nor golf and can be purchased for as little as $25,000. Which is the real bargain?

If you answered the most expensive lake lots, you'd be correct. Even though they are the most costly, the houses built on them will appreciate fastest in value, because they have the most desired location. (The next best lots are the view or golf lots, for the same reason.)

Unfortunately, I have seen people buy the cheapest lots (in our example, those without water, view, or golf), acting on the belief they were saving money. Then they put up a huge luxury home. Their idea was that as long as they were "close to" the desired features, it was good enough. On a limited budget, they chose to go for a bigger, better house over a better location.

Mistake! After their home was built, they always regretted not having the nicer lot and envied their neighbors who had views, water, or golf access. And later on, they had the hardest time reselling because, in effect, they had "overbuilt" for their lot. A tiny cottage on the lowest-priced lot would be fine; a big, fat house was just too much.

TIP

When buying a lot, the most important rule is location comes first.

I'm emphasizing this because so many people make this mistake, even after being told about it. If you want further proof, check out any new development of homes today. Typically you'll find huge homes on postage stamp lots. Why is the house so big and the lot so small?

The reason is that, as Will Rogers said about land, "They ain't making any more of it!" Land is precious, and costs are high. In some areas today, the cost of the lot is more expensive than the cost of the home you put on it!

Faced with this reality, many people delude themselves into thinking they can get by with less of a lot (or a poorer location), just as long as they can have a big house. But that means they are close to their neighbors and can hear loud music or even conversations. Or when they go into their yard, their neighbors are peering at them from their big houses. But worst of all, when it's time to sell, buyers shun these properties, instead looking for better located homes.

Don't fall into the trap of holding back when you buy your lot. Make getting the best lot the highest priority you have. We'll see ways to save loads of money elsewhere as we move along, but the lot is *not* the place to scrimp.

What Kind of Home Do You Want to Put on Your Lot?

Before you buy your lot, even before you begin looking, it's helpful to get a handle on just what you want from your lot. By knowing your real desires and needs, you can eliminate a good deal of wasted effort and can narrow your search to the most likely areas. Here are some questions you need to ask yourself:

LOT-BUYING QUESTIONNAIRE

1. Will the home be your primary or vacation residence?

   _____

2. Do you want to live in the country, the suburbs, or the city?

   _____

3. Do you need to be near an airport?   [   ] Yes [   ] No

4. Do you need a large home for a big family, or will a small one do?

   _____

5. Do you want to have a big picture window view? [   ] Yes [   ] No

6. If so, a view of what? River, lake, golf course, mountain, or something else?

   _____

7. Do you need to be near services (such as a senior center, hospital, medical clinics, and so on)?   [   ] Yes [   ] No

8. Do you need to be near ground transport such as taxis, buses, trains, or rapid transit?   [   ] Yes [   ] No

9. Do you want community activities such as golf, tennis, or swimming?   [   ] Yes [   ] No

10. Are you willing to make the effort necessary to find a good lot?
          [   ] Yes [   ] No

How you answer the above questions will lead you to where you're most likely to find a suitable lot. Let's consider some of the possible answers you might give and what they signify.

Will the Home Be Your Primary or Vacation Residence?

If it's your main house, then most likely you'll be willing to spend more on it. You'll also want to be sure that it's big enough to accommodate your entire family for full-time living. And, perhaps most importantly, you'll want it to be near where you work.

On the other hand, if it's to be your vacation home, then you'll use it infrequently and should be willing to accept compromises. You might be willing to put up with a smaller size and more Spartan surroundings. And you might be willing to give up some conveniences, such as being close to rapid transit.

TRAP

Beware of getting a big mortgage to pay for your vacation home. You'll tire of making that big mortgage payment long before you tire of the home. Plan your budget so that the vacation home doesn't take a big bite out of your income and you'll enjoy it far more.

What Facilities Must You Be Near?

If health is an issue, you will want to be located near doctors and a hospital. If this is your retirement home, then being near a senior center and senior activities would be a plus.

On the other hand, if you're still working, you will want to be sure you have access to rapid transit or to throughways so you can easily get back and forth to work. And being near an airport can be vital. (Many self-employed people can live just about anywhere there's an airport, a phone/Internet line, and Federal Express!) And if you have children, being in a good school district will be a big issue (see below).

What about leisure activities? Whether it's your main home or a vacation home, you may want to have access to your favorite sport. Are you a golfer? Do you love tennis? What about swimming or boating? If these are important to you, then finding a lot in an area that provides them will be of critical importance.

Do You Want a Lot with a View?

What about a house with a view? For some this is an absolute necessity. In fact, it's their main reason for wanting to build a home. But be sure you define the view you want. If it's of water, is a lake a necessity or will ocean or stream do? If it's just a bucolic setting, then will any woodsy lot be sufficient? Do you just want open space—what about a golf course view?

Do You Need a Big Building Site on the Lot?

Some lots are huge, but the buildable area is small. Do you love a second-story home, or are you looking for a place without stairs? For the former, a smaller building site will do. For the latter, you'll need a bigger one.

And on it goes—by narrowing it down to just what you want, you can soon determine just where to look.

TRAP

Don't begin by worrying about costs. If your heart is set on having a home on the water, don't give up because you imagine this will be too expensive. Building your own home is too much effort to end up with something you really don't like. Sometimes it's better to keep looking than to settle for second best.

Where Do You Look?

By now you should have narrowed your search. If you want a getaway vacation place, you obviously won't be looking near downtown. And you won't check out the woods if you want a place that's near urban activities.

The first place to search is the Internet. There are hundreds of Web sites devoted to listed property, including lots. Further, the chambers of commerce, county commissions, state promotional boards, and similar organizations have Web sites that will give you clues about what you're likely to find in their area. You can save yourself an enormous amount of time and energy by looking first on the Web.

Web Sites for Home Builders

Since Web sites change constantly, your best bet is to check out search engines with links to as many home building products as possible. Those are the places to search if you want to find out who makes a sink or cabinet, a truss, or a prefab bathroom. Also you'll find references to contractors, associations, and architects.

SEARCH ENGINES

www.yahoo.com

www.excite.com

www.lycos.com

Search words that are helpful include:

Build your own home

Home

Home building

Home shows

Home design

House plans

HELPFUL WEB SITES

www.nahb.com National Association of Home Builders (NAHB). Primarily for contractors, but contains much useful information on new developments in the field of construction. Check out the NAHB Research Center for publications and information on all aspects of building.

www.kuhnsbros.com Kuhns Brothers log construction. Includes prices, plans, and instructional materials.

www.lindal.com Lindal cedar homes and sunrooms. Gives virtual tours of homes they've built. Very helpful in designing your own home.

www.taunton.com Taunton Press books, tapes, and videos on virtually every area of home building, with the emphasis on doing it yourself.

www.thisoldhouse.com The Web site for the *This Old House* show seen on both public television and the Learning Channel. Includes tips from the shows on virtually every aspect of home renovation. Sells videos and books.

www.buildingonline.com and *www.build.com* A source for building materials and contractors. Will connect you to other Web sites in the field.

www.bydesign-ink.com A large list of home design plans. Will modify plans to suit your specific needs, online.

www.plan-publishers.com Lets you purchase house plans either in hard-copy form or in AutoCad so you can modify them.

Once you've narrowed your search to one or even a couple of areas, go there. Your first stop should be a real estate office in the area. Talk to the broker (not the salesperson). You can learn more about an area in an hour talking to a local real estate agent than you can by driving around the same area for days.

Ask the broker to show you suitable lots, but don't feel you must buy those you are shown. Indeed, if you don't see exactly what you want, thank the broker and look elsewhere. Keep in mind that unlike built homes, lots sometimes are not put on the Multiple Listing Service. Sometimes brokers keep lot listings to themselves. That means you may need to check with several brokers.

TIP

Once you find an area you like, go back several times. If possible, rent a home or apartment in the area you are considering. See how well you really do like living there. Spending a few nights can give you a completely different perspective from just visiting for a day.

Also check out lots that are for sale by owners (FSBOs). Lots are much harder to sell than homes. This means that owners will sometimes give up on agents after trying to sell for 6 months or a year and may be attempting to sell on their own. Check local papers for ads and also drive the area looking for signs.

For more information on the actual purchase, I suggest you look at my book *Power Tips When Buying a Home* (McGraw-Hill, New York, 2000).

Check Out the Schools, the Crime Statistics, and the Attractiveness of the Neighborhood

The quality of the neighborhood is just as important when buying a lot as when buying a built home. After all, once you finish construction and move in, you want to be sure that it's a good place to live. You'll want to know the answers to these questions.

1. Are the Nearby Schools Good?

The single most important factor in determining price appreciation in most residential areas is school quality. Homes within reach of good schools go up in value. Those that feed into poor schools languish or may even decline in value. Check with the local school board for how well the schools do on state and national scholastic tests. You want schools in higher than the 50th percentile—and even better, higher than the 70th. Much of this information is available online.

2. Is the Area Relatively Free from Crime?

Although crime isn't as a big a consideration as it once was, it's still present in the back of most peoples' minds. Call the public affairs officer of the local police department or sheriff's office. He or she can provide you with statistical information on the number of crimes by type and location, often down to the very block the lot you are considering is on!

Don't just be concerned about absolute numbers. Every area has some crime. Ask how the local crime rates compare with state, regional, and national levels.

TRAP

When buying in a rural area, don't assume that the crime rate is automatically lower than for the city. Some rural areas have very high crime rates.

3.   Are There Any Local or Regional Drawbacks?

It's amazing how many toxic dump sites are located out in the most beautiful, wooded areas. Buying a lot close to one can be the kiss of death, financially and from a health perspective.

Sometimes you can be in a perfectly wonderful rural setting, only to learn that a maximum security state prison is only a heartbeat away. Do you really want to live next to a prison?

Sometimes the land itself is the problem. Is it basically swampland that can't be built upon? Are there other problems with it, such as shifting soil?

Ask specific questions of agents and sellers. They have a responsibility to tell you of any drawbacks to the region, else they could be liable if you buy and later discover something that could have influenced your purchase decision. But be double safe by checking out the area with local building and planning departments, which are usually very forthright about any problems.

5

Is the Lot Buildable?

I recently was shown a lot that covered nearly 3 acres of hillside. The sellers were anxious to sell and pointed out a lovely brook as well as the old oak trees scattered here and there. But my first question was, "Where's the building site?"

The problem was that the entire 3 acres was on steeply sloping land. There were no large level areas. If I wanted to build a home on the lot, I'd have to do it on stilts! (Something that can be done, but that is very expensive.)

TIP

A gentle slope often means good drainage, ease in putting in a basement, and, perhaps, even a view. It's steep slopes you should be concerned about.

Are There Utilities?

When you buy an already built home, you just assume that it's hooked up to water, power, sewer, and so on. Don't make that assumption when you buy a lot.

Lots may or may not have utilities. And even if they do, often those utilities only come to the edge of the lot, or perhaps to the center of a nearby street. You may have to pull them from that location all the way to your building site, an expensive proposition.

Be sure you check out:

Electricity

Potable water

Gas (natural)

Sewer

Cable TV

Phone

If there are no utilities, find out how far it is to them and what the cost would be to drag them to the lot. You can call the utility companies for this information.

TRAP

Be wary of relying on a seller's estimates for the price of dragging in utilities. Sellers are notorious for underestimating how much it will actually cost.

What About Septic Systems?

In rural areas you may discover that while electricity and phone are available at the lot, there are no sewer or gas hookups. Gas is usually no problem, as propane dealers tend to flourish in such areas and can deliver it to you in tanks. Just be sure to find out how much it will be for a propane tank of at least 250 gallons. (Some propane companies supply the tank free if you buy their gas.) Not having sewer service, however, can be a big headache.

If there's no sewer, then the most common method of disposing of waste is a septic system. It's important that you understand at least the basics of a septic system because it could impact enormously on your lot choice. (Figure 5-1.)

The septic system has two parts: a tank and a leach field. The tank size will be determined by how many bathrooms and bedrooms your home has. The more bathrooms and bedrooms, the bigger the tank. Typically tanks of between 1200 and 1500 gallons are used for a two-bathroom three-bedroom house. The tank is buried in the ground near your house and doesn't take up much room.

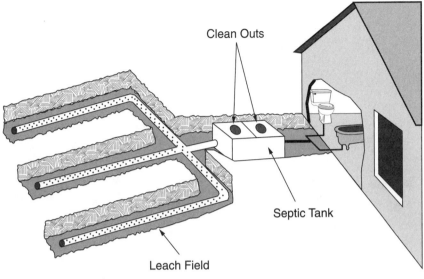

Clean Outs

Septic Tank

Leach Field

Figure 5-1. Septic System

The real problem is the leach field. While the tank holds solid waste, some of which slowly decays while other parts must be pumped out every few years, liquid waste must be allowed to leach into the ground. This means that you will need a system of pipes with small holes in them that allow the "gray water" to seep into the earth.

The leach field must cover an area large enough to allow the ground to absorb all the gray water the septic system delivers to it, and therein lies the problem. Is the lot big enough for the leach field?

You will need to have the soil tested for its ability to absorb moisture. (The building department will usually require this.) Good, friable soil may require a leach field that is only 20 feet by 30 feet. Soil in wet climates may require a much bigger field. And in some areas that are swampy, no leach field may be possible, making the land unbuildable.

Thus, if you are using a septic system, your lot will have to be large enough to accommodate not only your home, but also your septic tank and leach field. Keep in mind that you will also have setbacks from the front, side, and rear (to keep uniform distances between the property line and buildings) and that there may be easements granted to utilities (such as a power company) running along the land. Thus, although the lot appears to be big enough for the septic system, that does not guarantee it actually is. If your lot is small, you may need a waste engineer to plot everything out for you, just to be sure.

TRAP

Some building departments are now refusing to grant permits to lot owners unless they have enough room for both a primary and a secondary leach field. The primary one is what you build for your septic system. However, if it becomes plugged up (by solid waste because you didn't remember to have your tank cleaned every few years), the secondary is available. This is a plot of land large enough to accommodate an entirely new leach field. Thus, you need enough land for two, not just one!

Will You Need a Lot Survey?

A lot survey tells you the true boundaries of your land. It requires that a surveyor come out and mark the property line. (The cost for a simple survey is usually only a few hundred dollars.) A survey should be done whenever you buy a bare lot, whether it be out in the country or in the heart of the city.

The reason you need a survey, besides helping you to plot the location of your septic system, is so that you'll know just how much land you're getting and where it's located.

TRAP

Don't rely on fences to establish property lines. A fence can be put up anywhere—sometimes it's on the property line, and sometimes it's 10 feet over.

Sometimes a survey is required for title insurance and for a mortgage, but not always. Even when not required, however, you should order it for your own peace of mind. For example, a neighbor's house might be encroaching on your land. This boundary issue could cost thousands in attorney fees to eventually settle. Thus, you would want the seller to handle it before you bought. Or if it couldn't be settled, perhaps you wouldn't want the lot at all.

Are There Any Building Restrictions?

In the old days you simply sited where you wanted your house and began construction. Today, however, you must get permission before you break ground. There are at least three jurisdictions that you will want to check on before buying the lot to see if there are restrictions.

1. Check with the Planning Department

Virtually all areas of the country have a designated plan for residential areas. That may include such things as restricting homes to only one story or only two. It could require a cement driveway. It might even require that all lots be fenced to a height of 5 feet.

If you're planning on building a two-story building on land that is restricted to one-story structures, you will be in trouble. The same may be true if you're planning on a long gravel driveway, only to discover it will cost you an extra $20,000 to make it out of cement.

TRAP

Be sure to ascertain that the zoning is correct for your lot and area. You want single-family residential. If it's anything else, you might find a condo or even a strip mall suddenly going up next to your lot!

The county, city, or township planning department is usually located near city hall. A quick call to the city offices will tell you where it's located, and a few minutes spent there checking out the central plan for the lot you're considering will be time well spent.

2. Check with Any Homeowners Association

Planned communities are becoming the rule rather than the exception these days. And these have homeowners associations (HOAs) which have their own restrictions. For example, the HOA may require that you put a stucco exterior on your home. Or that you use no stucco, but instead use wood. Or that no windows or doors be larger than a certain size. Or that the roofs all be tile...or wood...or composition shingle. Or that the house be no less than 2000 square feet...

The restrictions are endless. Be sure that you can live with them.

TIP

Many of the restrictions for lots with HOAs (as well as for lots without them) are found in the covenants, conditions, and restrictions (CC&Rs) that run with the land. These will be part of any title insurance search. Read them carefully, as you will be bound by them.

3. Check with the Building Department

Most building departments rely on the Uniform Building Code (UBC) for construction. But in some areas the department's requirements may exceed or be different from the UBC. For example, on low land, 2 × 4 studs are commonly used for exterior walls. In mountain building, however, often the studs must be 2 × 6 both for strength to accommodate snow load and for thickness to accommodate extra insulation. In desert areas, sometimes brick or cement walls are desired. All this influences how you will be allowed to build on your lot and determines your extra costs.

Similarly, in warm climates, simple low-sloping and inexpensive roofs may be the rule. But in snow country, heavy peaked roofs often engineered to withstand 100 to 200 pounds per square foot of snow load are required. These heavier roofs can easily add $10,000 to $20,000 to the cost of building a home, something that you may want to take into consideration when buying a lot in a particular area. (For example, at a 5000-foot elevation you may need an expensive snow load roof; at 3500 you might not, because heavy snow doesn't normally fall that low.)

The building department is usually located near the planning department offices. Often you can check with them about any special requirements at the same time. Be sure to ask them about what's required for a sewer system in your area.

Will You Have a View Tomorrow?

Many people buy lots because of the terrific views they offer, and then situate their homes to take advantage of the view. There's nothing wrong with this, as long as you consider the long picture. What if over the next 5, 10, or even 20 years, trees on your neighbor's lot grow from the small seedlings they are today to 100-foot giants, obscuring your view? Will you be just as happy looking at the side of your neighbor's trees as you were looking at a distant mountain or lake?

TRAP

In most states there is "no right to a view." That means that your right to a view extends only as far as your property line. If a neighbor's trees grow tall and obscure your view, you may have no legal grounds to complain.

This is one of the advantages of buying a home on a slope. If you're up high, the chances are not as great that the neighbor down below will be able to obscure your view. However, keep in mind that many types of trees grow very tall. It may take years, but over time they can obscure your view.

TIP

In most areas the height of a fence, whether made of wood, metal, or living trees, is limited, typically to 5 or 6 feet. Your neighbor usually cannot construct a "living fence" of trees as a "wall" if the trees grow above the legal height of a fence and obstruct your view. And you can't do the same thing to your neighbor

Does Your Lot Have Trees?

Trees have value. Lots with trees are considered better than lots that are treeless. Besides, with established trees you don't have to do as much landscaping later on. And they look good.

I wouldn't necessarily pay much more for a lot with trees on it; but if I had a choice between two lots, one with trees and one without, I'd choose the one with trees.

Does Your Lot Have Good Soil?

Good soil means that it will hold up the structure of your home, won't get saturated in wet weather and expand, won't contract in dry weather, and will allow moisture to drain through it at a reasonably good rate. Very few lots have soil that's perfect in all these areas.

Usually soil has one or more drawbacks. It could be expansive clay, increasing and decreasing in volume depending on the water content. That means that it's constantly trying to crack your foundation.

Or there could be a ledge of stone or silt below ground level which could affect the soils load-bearing capabilities. Or the soil could be saturated with water, as in a swampy area, and be unfit for building.

Or it could be liquefied, which means that it's essentially sand that moves. If this is the case and the lot happens to be in earthquake country, building could be almost impossible, as any quake would cause major ground shifting.

Or there could be some other soil condition, from having an underground river drain through the lot to having huge boulders that would have to be dynamited in order to prepare a building site. All of which is to say that a soil inspection, including test borings and ground samplings by an engineer if necessary, is a must.

TIP

A soil inspection is now considered almost automatic when buying a lot. It should be written into the contract as a contingency, so that if the results turn out bad, you have the option of not approving and of walking away with your deposit. (You, of course, would normally pay for the inspection.)

There are many different types of soil you will encounter. Here's a list indicating the difficulty involved in excavation and in use for a leach field. Remember, be sure to get a soil analysis *before* buying or building:

SOIL UTILITY

Soil	Difficulty in excavation	Leach field
Boulders and rocks	May require blasting	Fair to bad
Gravel	Easy to average	Good to fair*
Clay	Average†	Poor†
Silt	Average to difficult†	Poor†
Organics (peat)	Difficult‡	Bad

*Depends on how much silt is in the gravel and what kind of soil is below it. If there's water below the gravel and you're using a well, you may not be able to use a leach field.

†Depends on the moisture content. If it's greater than 40 percent, the soil may be unable to support a leach field (poor drainage) or a foundation (the soil will expand with wet weather and contract with dry, causing the foundation to crack.)

‡May not support a foundation—the house could sink.

Can You Sink a Well?

If there's no water utility, you'll have to drill. But will the lot support a well? The questions to answer are how deep is the water, is it pure, and is there enough room on the lot for both a well and a septic system?

If you're going to need a well, it's a good idea to get expert advice. Usually in such areas there are companies that specialize in drilling wells. They can be of great help.

TRAP

 Don't use a well unless the water is regularly tested and it comes out clean. You want to test for both bacteria (usually fecal material) and toxics (such as arsenic and heavy metals).

Get the Seller to Warrant the Lot

The last thing you want to do is to buy a lot and then find that it is unbuildable. To avoid this problem, savvy buyers get the sellers to warrant the buildability of the lot. There are several ways to do this.

Perhaps the most effective is to refuse to close escrow on the purchase until you get building department approval for construction. For example, you have a clause written by your agent or attorney which specifies that you do not have to go through with the purchase until you get the necessary building approvals. Of course, this may take time and you may want a long escrow, 3 to 6 months. This is not that unusual when buying bare land.

On the other hand, the seller may want to close escrow immediately and, perhaps because you're getting such a good price, you decide to go along. You may want a clause inserted in which the seller warrants that the lot is buildable and agrees to a rescission of the deal if the lot proves not to be. (The seller has to give back your money and take back the lot.) The problem here is that about the only way to enforce such a clause is to go to court, and that could take years and ultimately cost a great deal of money.

We are all used to believing that when building a home, you start with the foundation. That's not true. You start with the lot. If you get a good buildable lot, then you're on your way to constructing a good home.

6

Hiring a Contractor

There are two ways of constructing your own home. One way is to hire a general contractor to do all the work for you. The GC will handle everything, and you will never get your hands dirty. You won't save much if any money (over buying a ready-built home), but you will get a home closer to what you really want than ready-built, and you'll have a ball making most of the design decisions.

The other way of building a home is to be your own contractor. You'll save money, loads of it, get even closer to exactly what you want—and also have a ball doing it. We'll discuss being your own contractor in the next chapter. For now, however, let's consider what you should look out for when hiring a general contractor.

What Does the Contractor Do?

There are two types of contractors on a job, the general contractor and the subcontractors. When you hire the GC, he or she then takes care of all the other hiring. You only need to hire one person.

The GC is the overall coordinator of the job. He or she follows the work through from start to finish and oversees all the big jobs as well as the tiniest details. This is the person who sees to it that *all* the work is done.

DUTIES OF A GENERAL CONTRACTOR

- Supervise all phases of work and see that the plans are carried out
- Hire, supervise, and pay subcontractors
- Buy all materials necessary to finish the job

- Coordinate all cleanup
- Deal with building department inspectors
- Get approvals from the building department
- Provide worker's compensation insurance

A sub (subcontractor) is a specialist such as a mason, plumber, carpenter, or electrician who works for and under the general contractor. A subcontractor is normally licensed in his or her specialty. (We'll look into hiring subcontractors in the next chapter.)

Where Do I Find a Good General Contractor?

You shouldn't have any trouble finding a GC to build your home for you. However, I don't recommend simply picking someone out of the phone book. Rather, I rely heavily on recommendations.

If you know of people who have recently built a home, check with them. Ask them how they liked their contractor. Typically these people will either rave over the wonderful job done or rant at the terrible experience they had. It can tell you a lot.

Another source of recommendations is materials suppliers such as lumberyards. Often if you strike up a conversation with someone there, you can quickly find out who the top builders in the area are.

Be aware that there's a long learning curve involved with being a GC. After builders get their contracting license, they will typically spend a few years struggling to find work. They may put up their own spec buildings. Generally, this level of contractor is hungry and will give you a lower bid.

Once the contractors establish themselves in an area, they usually can count on referral business (from satisfied clients). This level of contractor will usually charge more. On the other hand, you'll be getting experienced workmanship.

Finally, there are the savvy old contractors who have been out there doing this most of their lives. If they were good at it, they have a golden reputation. Everyone knows them and raves about them. This level of contractor usually (but not always) charges the most. But then again, as the old saying goes, you usually get what you pay for.

What Should I Look For in a GC?

When you meet GCs, check them out. While they will ask you questions about your job, be sure that you ask them specific questions to help you determine if they're right for you.

Questions to Ask a GC

Question 1: "Have You Built Homes Before and Do You Have References I Can Contact?" Once you've located a contractor, be sure to ask him what jobs he's currently working on and if you can go over and check them out. See what the work looks like. Does it seem to be well constructed? More important, contact the owner and ask how things are going. You'll usually get a strong opinion, one way or another

Ask for past references. Contractors will often have a list of homes they've previously built, with the names and phone numbers of the owners. Check them out.

TIP

Always check out references. Too many people assume that just because a GC can supply references, he or she must be good. That's not always the case. Many times the references will tell you horror stories that will give you goose bumps. But you won't know until you make the call.

Question 2: "Are You Licensed?" All states license contractors. However, not everyone who wants to work for you will have a license. Should you insist on only hiring licensed people?

When hiring a GC the answer is Yes. There are good reasons for this:

- You can call the state licensing board and find out if there are complaints against the contractor or if his or her license has been revoked or suspended.
- If the contractor messes up and doesn't do a good job, you can sue to recover damages more easily. (The presumption is that a licensed contractor knows what he or she is doing.)

- If you have a disagreement with the contractor, you can threaten to file a complaint with the state licensing board, and that will sometimes get you what you want.

TRAP

Just because the state licenses the contractor doesn't mean the state does a good job of policing. In many states the licensing board is lax and only takes action in the most severe circumstances and only after repeated complaints. Further, in many states the complaints against contractors are not made easily available to the public. Just because a contractor has a license is not a guarantee of good service.

Question 3: "Can You Post a Performance Bond?"   A performance bond promises that if the GC can't finish the job, the bonding company will step in and see to it that the job is completed, up to the amount of money of the bond.

Getting a bond is costly, often as much as 5 percent of the cost of the job. It also involves a lot of paperwork and hassle. As a result, many contractors will refuse to take a residential job where a performance bond is required.

That's okay. I don't usually require the GC to post a performance bond. I just want to know that he or she has the track record and solvency to get one. Only top contractors can post performance bonds.

Question 4: "Do You Have Worker's Compensation Insurance?" People get injured on the job all the time. All construction carries with it some degree of hazard. Therefore, you want to be sure that the contractor carries insurance to cover injuries to his or her workers. This is usually in the form of privately issued state worker's compensation.

TIP

Be sure to ask to see the current worker's comp policy. Just having a contractor tell you he or she has it isn't enough. You must see the actual policy and check the dates to be sure it's in force.

Question 5: "Can You Give Me a Firm, Written Bid?" It's important to remember that you're not building a rocket ship. You're simply building a home, and presumably the GC has done this many times before. Therefore, there's no reason that once you provide a complete set of plans and specs, you shouldn't be given a firm bid (see Chapters 8 and 9). A firm, written bid includes a bottom-line figure: The job will cost $20,000 or $50,000 or $100,000 or whatever.

Some contractors will prefer to give you a bid for "time and materials." In other words, they will take the job and you pay them so much an hour plus the cost of the materials required. Avoid this like the plague.

TRAP

When you hire someone for time and materials, it is an open-ended contract, and you really have no idea how much it will eventually cost you. This is the way that the government pays companies to build rocket ships; since it's never been done before—it's new and untested—the company will only do the work based on time and materials. And, of course, you have heard of how these sort of deals always save the government money, right?

A contractor who insists on being paid by time and materials and is unwilling to give you a firm, written bottom-line bid is usually one who is inexperienced. A contractor who has been in the business awhile will have an excellent sense of what things will cost and should have no trouble coming up with a bottom-line bid.

TRAP

When you're paying time and materials, there's no incentive on the part of the contractor to finish quickly or to use materials sparingly. Indeed, the incentives are in the other direction.

Question 6: "Can You Give Me a Start and Finish Date?" The start date is when the actual work will begin. Oftentimes it just means the day that the materials will arrive, but at least you'll know that the project is beginning.

A finish date is the date by which you can expect the project to be completed. For example, by September 15 all work will be done and signed off by the building department (if appropriate).

Contractors are loath to give start and particularly finish dates. The reason is that they make their living by doing several jobs simultaneously. They'll work a bit on yours, then a bit on mine, then a bit on someone else's.

There's nothing wrong with this if the jobs are small, such as renovation work. However, with whole-home construction, you want a crew to be on the job full time, at least until the shell (foundation, framing, sheathing, and roof) is completed.

The problem is that with contracting, it's either feast or famine. Either there's too much work or not enough. Thus, worrying about those famine times, contractors very frequently take on more work than they can comfortably handle to be sure that they have enough.

This results in unnecessary delays. The job takes twice as long as it should. And you're paying interest on your construction loan during that time. And if inclement weather sets in, it could cause more delays. Or worse, the weather could damage the work already completed.

What you need to be sure that the work gets done in a timely fashion is a written start and finish date. Although at one time I would sign a contract without a specified start date, I will not do so anymore. I've learned the hard way. Further, any good contractor will go along with this, particularly if I'm willing to give a few days or even weeks flex time on the back end.

TIP

Be flexible on finish dates. Ask the contractor when he or she is likely to be finished. Then add a couple of weeks to the finish date. If the contractor is still uncomfortable, add another week. You just want the work to be done in a timely fashion. If the contractor still refuses, you have to wonder why.

Do I Need a Contract?

When you hire a contractor, whether general or sub, you should have a written contract. This is not to say that you can't simply do it with a handshake. Many people do. Indeed, I've done it that way myself, particularly when the job was small and well defined and I knew the person with whom I was dealing. However, when building an entire home, a written contract is an absolute necessity.

TRAP

Even though you may be dealing with the most honest person in the world, any two people can honestly disagree about what each was supposed to do based on a verbal agreement made months earlier. Put it in writing so there can be no misunderstanding.

The reason you want a written contract is that it puts everything down in writing, so that later on the parties can't say they didn't know, they didn't understand, or they thought it was different. It's in writing, spelled out, and if the writing is clear, there shouldn't be any confusion.

A building contract:

- Explains what work is to be done
- When the work is to be done
- Who is going to do the work
- What happens if there's a problem

Further, later on if there should be trouble and you end up in court over a dispute with your contractor, the written contract will often be the deciding factor in who wins and who loses.

Where Do I Get the Contract?

The contractor will be ready to supply it. I've never known a contractor who wasn't ready to whip out a contract to have you sign as soon as you decided to do the work.

However, the contractor's contract might be a single sheet of paper with very little information on it other than the price of the job. That's really too little for you, especially with a job as big as a house. What you want is much more. What you want is a contract with all the things you need in it spelled out. A good contractor will have a multipage contract ready for you to sign. Read it over carefully and take it to your attorney for evaluation.

What If I Want to Make Changes or Use My Own Contract?

Using your own contract can present a problem. My experience with contractors is that while they may be excellent at the work they perform, often they are not very good at contracts. In other words, they know and understand their own contract, which may have been originally prepared for them by their attorney (or which they may have originally borrowed from another contractor). They've used it for years, know it thoroughly, and feel comfortable with it.

You whip out your own contract, however, and they'll look at it and wonder if they should sign or if they should have an attorney look at it. In short, they may suddenly become very suspicious of you. They may hem and haw, and they may finally say they'll take it along and have someone else look at it. It could be a long time before you hear from them again. In short, having your own contract can waste time and even result in a contractor refusing to work for you.

On the other hand, from your perspective, you should never use a contract that your attorney hasn't checked out. This applies especially to those generic contract forms found in stationery stores. (These contracts may not include clauses you need or may have clauses that are inappropriate for your job or for your area of the country.)

So how do you come up with a contract that will protect your rights and at the same time not scare away the contractor? My suggestion is that you carefully read over the contract given to you by the contractor to be sure it includes some minimum information. And then take it to your attorney, who may want to add additional clauses to protect you. You can then give this back to the contractor, who, if your contractor is smart, will have his or her own attorney check it out.

What Should Be in the Building Contract?

The contract should make things clear, not muddy them up. Here are 11 things I look for in any building contract that I sign.

1. Price

The whole price should be clearly spelled out. You give the builder a complete set of plans and specs (see Chapter 8), and he or she takes it and you don't hear anything for a week or two. Then, the builder comes back with a bid. The bid will probably break down the costs for materials and labor for a wide variety of items such as rough plumbing, heating, and so forth. But down at the bottom line there should be a total price for the entire job. The contract should include the bid with all the breakdowns as well as the final bottom-line price.

TIP

Many contracts specify that *you* will pay for all fees such as building permits, plan checks, and connections (to water, gas, sewer, etc.). Be aware that this is often *in addition* to the contract price.

TRAP

Most contracts specify that they are subject to an increase in price if you deviate in any way from the plans. You should negotiate a clause that says if you do want to change the plans, a new bid will be given for the change, not that it automatically reverts to time and materials charges.

2. Payment Schedule

When payment is due should be spelled out. Typically there will be a payment schedule. For example, the contractor may want 10 percent upon signing and the rest in increments as phases of the work are done.

Since your construction loan will also specify a payment schedule (when monies will be made available to you), be sure both schedules jibe. You don't want the contractor to be expecting 30 percent upon completion of framing and the construction contract calling for you to get only 20 percent. (See Chapter 11 for more on financing.)

A typical payment schedule might look like the following:

DISBURSEMENT SCHEDULE FOR CONSTRUCTION MORTGAGE FUNDS

WORK	DATE INSPECTED	APPROVED
Materials package		
Chimney		
Septic/sewer system		
Excavation		
Footings and foundation		
Slab		
Framing (wall and roof)		
Flooring		
Roofing		
Sheathing		
Windows and doors		
Exterior finish		
Rough plumbing		
Rough mechanical		
Rough electrical		
Flues		
Heater installed		
Insulation		
Drywall		
Cabinets		
Plumbing fixtures		
Countertops		
Painting interior		
Appliances		
Light fixtures		
Tile/floor covering		
Driveway		
Landscaping		
Finaled/holdback		

Typically, 10 percent of the cost of the work is retained until 30 days after completion. This is done to ensure against defective work that crops up later and also to ensure that there are no problems with mechanic's liens, described below. Always get this in your contract. Since this part is often a large part of the profit, it gives a big incentive to the GC to totally complete the job.

3. Start and Completion Date

As noted earlier, I consider this vital information. I believe that both dates should be specified. However, some contracts state that the work will be "substantially complete" by a certain date. This gives the contractor an edge in case most of the work is done, but a little bit of finish remains. I don't consider this unreasonable.

TRAP

When a job is finished can be a matter of some confusion. Is it when the contractor says he or she is done? Is it when a building inspector approves the work? Or is it when you say the job is done and file a "notice of completion"? A good contract will spell this out.

There can even be a penalty the contractor must pay in the event the entire job isn't finished on time (or if there is a completion schedule, if a designated portion of work is not finished on time). For example, for every day the job is late, the contractor will pay a penalty of $100.

Penalties are usually found in commercial contracts. Most residential home builders, aware that the owner may make changes along the way that can slow things down, will not agree to them. I don't consider this an important item in a residential building contract because it's usually very hard to enforce.

4. The Work to Be Done

This should be very specific. It should state that the home is to be built according to the building plans and spec sheet you've submitted. It should also indicate the level of completion the contractor is responsible for—just the shell, all the rough work, all the finish work, the complete job, or what? Be sure to specify all finish work (such as installing cabinets, appliances, plumbing, painting, and so on) that the contractor is responsible for, so that there can be no misunderstanding.

The contract should also specify who is to supply and pay for labor and materials (you, the lender, the contractor?). And it should indicate that all work is to be done in a workmanlike manner (according to current building standards).

In addition, it should specify that the materials used must match the spec sheet (which, it is hoped, you completed in great detail) right down to the nailing schedule. With regard to appliances such as heaters, air conditioners, sinks, and so on, everything should be specified down to the manufacturer of the product, the model numbers, even the color.

Finally, the contract should specify that the contractor is responsible for cleanup to be done during construction and after all the work is completed.

TRAP

Most contracts provide that you, not the contractor, will be responsible for unknown hazards that crop up (such as a sinkhole suddenly appearing in the backyard) and that delay work. This is only fair, but it is something to watch out for.

5. Who Has Approval?

Does the contractor have approval of the work? What about a building inspector? What about you? What is your recourse if you don't approve of the work? Can you withhold the final payment until you or an inspector approves? If the contractor refuses to (or can't) make good on work that you find below standard, can you then contract with someone else to do the work and subtract the cost from the contractor's payment?

Most GCs will not agree to this clause. To make it sweeter, you might include an arbitration condition—that if there's an argument about approval, it will eventually go to arbitration. The problem here is who is to do the arbitration? If it's a group of builders, those builders may side against you and with the contractor!

Another solution is to hire an independent building inspector to supervise the job. These inspectors are available in most areas. If both you and the GC can agree on an inspector, you're set. The only drawback is the additional cost, which can be substantial.

TIP

The usual inexpensive way to ensure reasonably good work is to make payment dependent on getting approval from the building department. While the inspectors do not always do a perfect job, at least they do usually check for minimal adherence to the building code.

This issue also touches on the matter of a mechanic's lien, which the contractor could file against you, discussed below.

6. Conditions to Be Maintained During Work

This is important if you're building in an urban setting or there is a strong homeowner's association. A neat, clean building site may be required of you. If that's the case, you want to be sure the contractor understands this and abides by the rules.

The contract should specify that work is to be cleaned up after each day and that no debris is to be left on the building site.

Many cities and counties also have specific ordinances with regard to noise and work. Some specify the work cannot commence, for example, before 7 in the morning or continue after 7 at night. You want to be sure the contract specifies that the contractor will follow all the appropriate ordinances.

7. How Will Changes Be Handled and Charged?

Remember from our earlier discussion the problems that can occur if you want to make later changes? If you do, how must you present them to the contractor (new plans, written notice, etc.), and how will the contractor charge you for them? Be wary of a charge by time and materials. Instead, look for a new bid on the work to be done so that you can decide *if* you actually want to go forward with it.

Also, a good contract will specify that the contractor can't change the materials or work without your written approval. If you don't have this clause, you might find that your tile roof is suddenly asphalt and rocks!

8. The Contractor Will Maintain Worker's Compensation Insurance at All Times

Be sure you see a current policy. You may also want to secure a policy of liability insurance, protecting yourself against accidents.

9. How Can the Contract Be Terminated?

What's going to happen if either you or the contractor decides that you can't move forward with the work? For example, the contractor starts and you suddenly lose your job. You're in a financial pinch, and you want the work stopped immediately. How much do you owe the contractor: the whole amount or only for work completed? This should be specified in advance.

10. Who Pays for Attorney's Fees?

Anything can go wrong, even when there's the best of intentions on both sides. If it does and one party sues the other, is the losing party going to be responsible for attorney's fees. If you win, you'll want this. If you lose, you won't.

11. Is There Binding Arbitration?

Do you want to be bound by arbitration, as some contracts specify? It could save you attorney's costs. On the other hand, it could keep you from suing if you feel you've been financially injured. And arbitration can be expensive.

Both attorney's fees and arbitration clauses are something your attorney should help you with.

When Should I Sign the Contract?

Don't be pressured to sign until you're absolutely sure it's just what you want. It's too late to reconsider *after* you've signed. Take the time to look the contract over in private and to have an attorney check it out.

You should be satisfied that:

- All the work you want done is included.
- The price is as agreed.
- You're comfortable with all the terms.

TRAP

Be wary of pressure put on you to sign quickly. Sometimes contractors will offer a discount if you sign right away. I've found that even if I wait a few days or even weeks and then say I'll sign, but only if I still can have the discount, I get it.

Never Make Advance Payments

Never, ever pay *before* the work is done. Don't get ahead of your payment schedule. Chances are you'll need approval from your lender to make payments anyway, and your lender won't approve them until it's satisfied the work is done. Nevertheless, if you at some point have the option of advance payment, turn aside. If you pay in advance, the chances are you may never get the job completed.

What Happens If You Don't Pay? (Mechanic's Liens)

You may not want to pay because you're unhappy with the workmanship. The walls are crooked; the window is cracked; the plumbing can't pass inspection. Should you pay anyway?

As long as my contract specified that the job was to be done in a workmanlike manner, I wouldn't. That, however, doesn't mean I wouldn't get in trouble with mechanic's liens.

In order to protect suppliers of labor and materials from owners who contract for work and then refuse to pay, every state has instituted mechanic's liens. These allow the supplier of labor or materials (the "mechanic") to place a lien on your property. This includes the contractor as well as the subs.

A lien is technically a money encumbrance that ties up your title. You won't be able to give clear title; in other words, you won't be able to sell your property until the lien is paid off. Further, in certain circumstances the lien holder could force the sale of your property in order to recover the amount you owe!

In short, mechanic's liens are nothing to fool around with.

Who Can Slap a Mechanic's Lien on Me?

The answer is anyone who is authorized (by you or your agent or representative) to supply labor and materials to your job. This has some frightening consequences, which seldom occur, but which can happen. *An example:* You hire a general contractor to do the job, which is completed, and you pay him. But he doesn't pay his subcontractors. They, then, can file a mechanic's lien against you and you might have to pay them, too. In other words, you could have to pay twice for the same work!

Or you're unsatisfied with the work and you tell the GC you won't pay him. He says he's sorry, but it's the fault of the subs. Of course, if you don't pay the GC, he can't pay the subs, and they then slap a mechanic's lien on you.

What's the Procedure for Slapping a Mechanic's Lien?

Each state prescribes the procedure to be used, but most are similar. There are usually two parts to a mechanic's lien, the notice and the lien itself.

The notice, also called the "prelim" or preliminary notice, often must be served to you before the lien can be filed. In California the minimum time is 20 days after you first receive the material or after labor is supplied. You must physically receive this notice, so most are sent by registered mail with return signature required.

Thus, sometimes when you start a job, you'll suddenly get a series of prelims from materials and labor suppliers. Don't panic! They are just notifying you that if later on you don't pay, they've already served you with notice and can proceed to slap a lien on you.

TIP

Getting a prelim lets you know who is working on your job and supplying materials. This can actually help you to check them out later on to be sure they were, in fact, paid.

There are time limits for filing a mechanic's lien. These relate to when the job is completed. Generally speaking, if you record a "notice of completion," something you may be wise to do (you can find one at a stationery store, or any escrow company can handle it for you), the subs and materials suppliers have a set period of time to file mechanic's liens—in California it's 30 days (60 days for the general contractor). If they aren't recorded by then, they will have no effect.

On the other hand, if you don't file a notice of completion, the time limit extends out. In California it is 60 days after work ends or 90 days after the whole project is completed (generally evidenced by a clearance from the building department).

Once the mechanic's lien is filed, the mechanic has a limited amount of time to start judicial action against you, usually 90 days. This means the mechanic must file against you (to have your property sold to pay off the lien) in court.

This rarely happens. Usually the threat is enough to make most owners pay up or at least seek a compromise or arbitration.

TRAP

Don't ignore mechanic's liens. Contact the sub or the materials supplier and try to explain what the problem is. Many times these people will be willing to wait, if they see their money coming. On the other hand, if they are the very ones who performed badly, then they may not care. After all, you'll probably see them in court one way or another fairly soon.

Are There Problems with Lenders and Mechanic's Liens?

For lenders, the big issue is order of precedence. In other words, which lien comes first. If a mechanic's lien is filed before a mortgage, then it has precedence. That means in any forced sale (for example, foreclosure) the mechanic's lien gets paid before the mortgage. For that reason lenders usually will not allow any materials to be delivered or work started until their mortgage (construction loan) is recorded. If you start work early, you might not get your financing!

Later on, after work has been completed, the lender may require that you produce lien releases (described below) before payments are made.

What Can I Do to Avoid Mechanic's Liens?

Obviously, you can pay your bills. But even more than that, to be sure that you're not being taken advantage of by an unscrupulous contractor, you can institute certain procedures to help make sure that payment has actually been received.

1. Get Lien Releases from All the Suppliers of Materials and Labor

Typically a contractor will round up all the subcontractors and get them to sign lien releases. Then he or she will hand them to you along with a bill for the work.

TRAP

Unless otherwise specified, all lien releases are conditional. In other words, they release you from a mechanic's lien provided the supplier of materials or labor gets paid. If you get the release and pay the general contractor and he or she, in turn, doesn't pay the subcontractors, you can still be slapped with a mechanic's lien! If your check doesn't clear the bank, you can still be slapped with a mechanic's lien.

TIP

Get an "unconditional" lien release. Suppliers of materials or labor normally will only give you this *after* they have, in fact, been paid (your check has cleared or you pay in cash). It states that no matter what, the mechanic waives rights to slap you with a lien.

2. Pay the Labor and Materials Suppliers Yourself

If you're concerned about handing over a big check to a contractor who must then pay subs and materials suppliers, pay them yourself. I have set up accounts at lumberyards or hardware stores that are billed directly to me. They are for a maximum amount of money, and the general contractor has the flexibility to go in and order whatever he or she needs. I get the bill, and I know if and when it's been paid since I pay it. I've had no problem with contractors working with me this way.

I have done this with subcontractors as well. Most GCs, however, don't like this procedure since it confuses who's really in charge, the GC or the person writing the check, me.

3. Get a Performance Bond

As described earlier, this assures that payment is made. However, as also noted, it adds to the cost of the job (as much as 5 percent or more), and many contractors simply can't get one or won't work with one.

The Bottom Line

Whether you hire a contractor to do all the work or you act as your own GC, be sure you check out everyone carefully. Building a house involves a lot of money, and you don't want any of it wasted.

7

Be Your Own Contractor

For many people, being their own contractor is a joy. For others, it is simply too big a challenge. If you're in the former group, take heed—as noted in the last chapter, you can expect to save 15 to 35 percent of the building costs being your own contractor. And since you're in charge, you'll get a home much closer to exactly what you want.

Sound okay? But can you really do it?

The answer is yes you can, even without hammering in a single nail. You can do all the decision work of the GC and hire subs to do all the physical work. (Of course, you can save even more by doing some of the physical work yourself.)

Can You Really Be Your Own General Contractor?

Can you handle it? Most people can. Usually, however, those who feel most confident about it are people who have had previous experience in building and in general are "handy." And from what I've seen, they usually succeed.

But beware of biting off more than you can chew. You may think you can do the work of a general contractor simply because you are largely unaware of what's actually involved. If you haven't previously worked with subcontractors and at least done some significant home repair or remodeling work, you should seriously consider hiring the services of someone to help you with the job.

TRAP

It takes time to do the work of the GC. You need to be constantly on the site supervising. Most people, however, can't take the time off from their regular work to do this. If you're going to be your own GC, be sure you allot enough time to do the necessary work.

What Will I Do When I'm My Own Contractor?

You'll need to do the following:

- Find subcontractors.
- Negotiate contracts with them.
- Direct and supervise their work.
- Be on call to accept materials deliveries.
- Inspect the job on regular occasions.
- Pay for materials and work.
- Deal with building inspectors.
- Provide worker's comp insurance.
- Do all the other work that a general contractor would do.

What's the Downside of Not Hiring a General Contractor?

If you hire a general contractor, presumably someone who's knowledgeable and experienced is doing the work. Thus you can count on a good job done efficiently.

Also, you can simply be a bystander and occasionally come by to watch the work progress. You don't need to get into the hassle of it. And best of all, when something goes wrong, there's a designated person at whom you can rant and rave! In short, you pay for having someone else do all the work and take all the blame.

On the other hand, you're paying big bucks for all this. So the question becomes, is hiring a GC worth it to me, or should I chance doing it myself?

Hire Someone to Help You Do the Work

If it is your first time out, I recommend that you hire a general contractor to *manage* the construction for you. This is different from hiring the GC to do the whole job.

When managing, the GC doesn't do everything. For example, he or she may just manage the pouring of the foundation, the framing, the sheathing, and the roofing of the house. Once the shell is thus finished, you can subcontract out the remainder or even do it yourself.

TIP

When you hire someone to help you with the GC work, be sure that person has a cell phone and keeps it nearby at all times. That way that person can contact you instantly with any problems. And you can contact the person with any instructions. I once bought a cell phone for a contractor so that I would be able to call him on the job. It was money well spent.

Must I Use a General Contractor to Help Me Manage the Job?

Many GCs will be willing to work on a management contract, particularly if they don't happen to be busy and if you agree to use their work crews. But expect their fee to be substantial.

One way to cut costs is to find a GC substitute. Usually the best person for this is an experienced carpenter.

A good carpenter is the key to building any home. He or she usually will know about foundations, framing, and roofing as well as sheathing and will be able to handle and supervise all this work. Often you can pay a carpenter something extra to be on the site and do the supervisory work as well as participate in the physical building of the home.

TIP

Sometimes carpenters will work for contractors part of the time and put up their own "spec" homes on their own time. Since they have built complete houses, they should have the knowledge to do the work for you—a good choice.

Where Do I Find a Carpenter-Manager?

If you're looking for an experienced carpenter to manage the work, chances are you'll have to search carefully. Carpenters don't usually advertise, nor will suppliers always know whom to recommend (although you can try asking suppliers who sometimes may know of a carpenter who's working his way up toward becoming a GC).

I've found that a good way to locate experienced carpenters is to stop by homes under construction. I usually stroll up and tell the work crew that I'm just admiring the building because I'm in the process of constructing my own home. I mention that I'm looking for subs and in particular a carpenter-manager. Usually at least one member of the crew will come forward to talk to me.

Sometimes the whole crew works exclusively for a particular GC and will not be able to make a recommendation. Other times the crew members will know about crews or individual carpenters who freelance. And who knows, sometimes the person you chance upon will himself or herself be the perfect candidate.

TRAP

When hiring a carpenter to help supervise the work, be sure this person won't be taking on more than he or she can handle. Ideally you want someone who has done some GC work before. If you are the person's first big job, it could be the blind leading the blind.

What About a Contract?

If you hire a carpenter-manager, you will certainly want to have a formal written agreement with this person. However, chances are that unless this person has done some extensive GC work, he or she won't have a ready-made contract. Or it will be one of the single pieces of paper that subs sometimes use for small jobs.

This won't do. You need a formal contract, and you should have an attorney draw it up. Yes, it will cost you a few extra bucks, but the peace of mind it brings will be worth it in the long run.

Be sure to check the previous chapter for questions to ask the carpenter and suggestions on what to include in the contract. Use this same technique when hiring subs.

Do You Need Worker's Comp?

If you hire a carpenter to supervise the work, more than likely he or she won't have worker's comp. Therefore, the responsibility is on you to carry it. Be aware that in today's workplace, many workers do not have health insurance. That means if they get injured on the job and there is no worker's compensation to cover the injury, their only recourse could be to sue you.

You can pick up a worker's comp policy from any major insurer. And while you're at it, see if you can get liability coverage to protect you in case someone does decide to sue you over the job.

Will a Lender Let Me Be My Own General Contractor?

We'll discuss financing in detail in Chapter 11. But this is an important question to answer now. As part of getting a construction loan, any lender is going to want to be convinced that the project has an excellent chance of being successfully completed. That means someone competent and knowledgeable is in charge. Indeed, one of the requirements of getting construction financing will be to identify the GC you are using. And the lender may require the GC to submit his or her license as well as a history of previous projects.

Now, however, you want to be your own GC. What's the lender to think?

It's important to understand that lenders are in the business of making loans. If you can demonstrate you can complete the project and pay back the loan, most won't care who does it, you or a licensed GC. Demonstrating your competence, however, is the key.

The lender may demand to know your background. How many previous homes have you successfully built? If the answer is zero, you're going to need to show that you've got a competent carpenter (or even a GC) managing the work for you. Even so, some lenders will still balk, and you may have to shop around to get financing when you do the project yourself.

Don't get discouraged, however. There are many, many lenders, and the competition to lend money is fierce. Chances are there are several that will be willing to work with you.

Of course, you could always pay cash for the construction. Again, see Chapter 11 for details on how to do this.

Should I Do Some of the Work Myself?

This, of course, is the way to save the most money, particularly if you do the high-cost work yourself. In the first house I built, I hired a GC to manage putting up the shell. Then I hired subs to handle the insulation, drywall, rough plumbing, electrical, and heating and air. But my sons and I physically did all the finish work ourselves, including the woodworking (hanging doors, placing molding), finish flooring, and so on. Since as much as half of the cost of construction can be in the finish work, the savings were enormous.

Can I Do Some of the Work Myself?

The other side of the coin is, can you do the work successfully? Some jobs, such as plastering or woodworking, require high levels of skill.

Other jobs, such as framing and pouring concrete, require great strength and endurance. And all the work involved requires that you do a workmanlike job so the results look good.

TRAP

You won't save a dime if you physically do the work yourself and the outcome looks bad. In that case, you'll probably have to hire someone to rip out what you did and then do it correctly, which will end up costing more than if you had a pro do it right the first time.

If this is your first home, I suggest you don't do any of the work yourself (unless, of course, you're in the trades). Save the money by doing most of the management yourself and by hiring subs. Let them do what they do best. The home will get built faster and end up looking professionally done.

On the other hand, if you've already built a home or have some direct construction experience, then by all means jump in and do the work yourself. You'll enjoy it, and the house will have added meaning for you.

TIP

The first time out, be a manager—and learn. The next time you can do much of the physical work yourself if you want to.

How Do I Hire Subcontractors?

The subcontractors are the people who actually do the work of building the house. They include the following:

SUBCONTRACTORS YOU MAY USE

Electrical

Plumbing

Masonry

Insulation

Roofing

Decking

Drywall

Plaster/texture

Excavation

Framing

The first question is, where do I find all of these people? The answer is that, with the exception of carpenters, most will advertise. That means they will have ads in the yellow pages, on the Internet, sometimes even in local newspapers. Of course, when you pick someone at random, you risk getting a bad apple as well as a good one.

A better source of information is a recommendation. If you have a GC or carpenter-manager, that person should be able to come up with all the subs you'll need. Typically you'll be told, "Call Jack and Jane and tell them I recommended them." You'll make the contact and explain what you want, and you'll soon be getting a bid.

TIP

Good people know other good people. If you get one sub you know and like, chances are he or she can put you in contact with half a dozen others and very quickly you'll have a network of qualified, competent people. I know that each time I build, I immediately call people I know and ask for recommendations. They only tell me the very best subs out there.

If you don't know anyone who can get you started, check out the building suppliers. Usually they will have cards of various subs. Some even have a large bulletin board filled with the cards. Pick at least three in each area and interview them. You'll very quickly discover whom you like and whom you don't. (Go back to the last chapter for a list of questions to ask any contractor.)

TRAP

Too many people fail to check out recommendations. If I'm hiring a plumbing contractor, I'll go to the last couple of jobs he or she did and talk to the owners. Was the work up to professional standards? Were there problems once the water was turned on? Don't be shy about checking out the people who will build your home.

Do I Need a Contract with a Sub?

Yes you do. It needs to contain the same information that you wrote down for the GC. Again, check the last chapter for information on contracts. You'll also need to get bids. Check out Chapter 9 for getting accurate bids.

TIP

Get at least three bids on every job. Just as with GCs, you'll be astonished at the different prices you'll be quoted for the same work. Just be sure you give each bidder a final set of plans and specs so you can compare apples with apples.

8

Getting the Plans and Permissions

Just as you can't build your home without a set of plans, you can't build it without permission from the building and planning departments of the local city or county. You may also need approval from the county's sanitation engineer, a homeowners association, or a land-use committee. You may even need to submit an environmental impact report, if you're building on land designated as a wildlife or other type of preserve. In short, before you start construction, be prepared to spend some time getting all the necessary "OKs."

But don't get discouraged. I've found that in almost all cases, the people from whom you must get approval will work with you and will help you jump through the various hoops. It's just a matter of being patient.

Be prepared, however, to change your plans. For example, you may want to put in big bay windows facing a view on one side of your home. However, the building department may require that the window area of your home be no more than 15 percent of the square footage, in order to make the home energy-compliant. You either remove some of your bay windows or cut down on the window space in other rooms. (Every room in the house, with the exception of hallways, bathrooms, and washrooms, is normally required to have a window for light and ventilation.)

TIP

Allow at least 3 months for all approvals of plans. It could, of course, be as short as a week or so. But if you run into objections, you may have to redo your plans

and resubmit them several times and to several different governing bodies. This can slow you down.

What Plans Will I Need?

You'll need a set of plans to show anyone from whom you're secur-
ing approval exactly what you're building. And your plans will need
to be clear enough for a builder to follow. Typically you'll need the
following:

PLANS REQUIRED TO BUILD A HOME

Plot plan.   This shows what the lot looks like, where all the setbacks and easements are, where the house will be placed, where
the leach field and septic tank will go (if you're using one), and
other important features. You can get a basic plot plan of your lot
from your surveyor and your architect. (Or you can draw it yourself.) Once you have the basic plot plan, you can sketch in where
everything goes. Be sure all measurements are accurate.

Elevations.   These are sketches showing how the house will look
from the outside. Usually at least four are used, one for each com-
pass direction. An architect (or you) can draw these.

Foundation plan.   This shows where the foundation goes. It
shows the depth, any piers used, slabs, and so forth. It should also
show the load-bearing requirements, so that the foundation will
be hefty enough to support the house. This plan also will show the
basement (if you have one), and it often shows the rough plumbing, if any of it is to go into or through the foundation.

Floor plan.   This is what most people think of when they visualize
a set of plans. It shows the dimensions of each floor; the headers
and beams to be used and their size and load; and the location of
the windows and doors, electrical outlets and switches, and heating and cooling vents and ducts. As well, it gives all the information necessary to rough in the house. Usually it takes an architect,
or at minimum a skilled draftsperson, to come up with a set of
floor plans from which a builder can work.

Detail sheet.   This is a cross section of the inside of the house
showing the materials used such as drywall, exterior sheathing,

cabinets, bricks, insulation, paneling, and so forth. There may be several detail sheets showing various portions of the home where it would otherwise be difficult to tell what was to be done. Usually an architect or draftsperson needs to create these.

Spec sheet. This simply lists all the materials, from wood to nails to appliances, that will be used in the home. You will probably need some help getting everything together, but you can make this up on your own.

Can I Draw the Plans Myself?

There is no one to say you can't, but you had better know all the conventions used with building plans. I have a friend who took a drafting course one semester in high school, and that was enough to allow her to draw plans that she used for successfully building a home from the ground up.

TRAP

If this is your first home, I suggest you don't do the plans yourself, but instead pay an architect or at least a skilled draftsperson to come up with a complete set of plans for you. Alternatively, you can buy a set of ready-made plans from magazines. Just be sure you have them adapted to your specific needs.

TIP

Remember, the only purpose of plans is to show what you want done. As long as you can get that across clearly, you've done the job.

A quick word about home-drawn plans and building department approval. I've never known a building department to refuse approval of home-drawn plans, regardless of the size of the project, if they were drawn correctly and clearly. Nobody says you must use a professional.

Can I Submit Ready-Made Plans?

Yes, but as I've noted above, be careful of using generic plans. While the building department may approve them, they may not fit your lot or purpose. I recently visited a home that an individual built from a set of purchased plans. The trouble was that the plans assumed the house would be on flat land. His lot, however, sloped, and so he had to modify his foundation. The result was that one side of the home stood high up in the air, something that defeated the design and made it look awkward.

What About Engineering?

Today virtually all home building plans must be "engineered." That means that a structural engineer has examined the plans and calculated the load-bearing requirements. Once you have your plans in hand (assuming your architect doesn't handle this for you), you take them to an engineering company (these companies advertise in the yellow pages) and have the company look them over.

The engineer will calculate the loads for walls, ceilings, decks, foundations, and so forth and then write in the minimum size wood, steel, concrete, or whatever that's required. Then the engineer will put his or her stamp on the plans. Most building departments today require full-house building plans to have engineering done before they will consider them.

Don't be worried about the cost, however. For a typical home without steel, the cost for engineering is usually only a few hundred dollars. Any steel or sophisticated construction, however, can run up the engineering costs significantly.

Who Needs to Approve My Plans?

It depends on where you live. If there's no HOA (homeowners association), you won't need its approval. If there is a HOA, almost certainly it will have an architectural committee and it will need to give its approval. There are several approvals you'll also need, including that of the HOA.

Homeowners Association Approval

Sometimes the hardest approval to get is from the HOA. Typically, you will need to submit at least a plot plan and elevations. You'll also need to submit such things as the exterior color, exterior materials, type of driveway, and so forth. Anything that your neighbors can see is usually within the purview of the HOA.

All too frequently, the HOA will shoot you down. It will want different colors or exterior materials, or there may be a height or square footage restriction.

What can you do if the HOA has ideas different from yours? Of course, you can ask the architectural committee to reconsider or appeal the decision to the full board. But if the organization is intent on maintaining rules of conformity (which it usually is), you may not be able to go forward with your project until you conform to the requirements. It can be a real surprise if this is the first time you're building within a HOA's jurisdiction.

Once you get homeowner's approval, if needed, your next step is usually the local planning department.

Planning Department Approval

The planning department enforces the CC&Rs (conditions, convenants, and restrictions) that run with the title to your property, as well as the local master plan, if there is one.

The CC&Rs restrict what can be done with your property. For example, they may specify the minimum amount of square feet that can be built on any floor of a building. You want to add a second floor of 500 square feet, but the CC&Rs specify that the minimum for a second floor is 800 square feet. Either you add more or you abandon the second floor.

There may be a local planning model that is often part of a master plan for your area. It specifies such things as the "setback," how far from the street and other houses your house may be, and even the maximum height of a building. You can easily get into trouble with these if you're not careful. For example, you want your home to butt right up to the side of your property. However, there is a 5-foot-minimum side-yard setback requirement. You can only come within 5 feet of the side property line.

TIP

You can always appeal the planning department's decision and try to get a "variance." This is a special exemp-
tion just for you. Normally you won't get a variance
approval unless you can demonstrate that your changes
won't be detrimental to neighbors or won't substantially alter the overall general plan. To be successful, you
often have to get all the affected neighbors to sign a
statement in favor of what you want to do, plus provide
the planning department with compelling reasons why
you should be allowed to move forward. You will also
have to pay a fee. Sometimes, in order to get a variance,
you will want to go over the head of the planning
department and take the entire matter to the full city
council. Obviously, much time and effort are involved.
And I would put your chances of success at less than
50:50, depending on the circumstances involved.

Once you get approval, your next step is the building department.

Building Department Approval

The building department enforces the local building code. Usually
the local building code is the UBC (Uniform Building Code) with
some local additions to make it stricter in certain ways. (For example, your area may have expansive soil, and so the local building
department may insist on deeper footings than the UBC specifies.)
The UBC is a comprehensive code for building construction used
throughout the United States. There are also codes for plumbing,
electrical, and so on.

TIP

I like to use the word "minimum" with regard to a building code because in some cases the code may not be as
strict as you would like. For example, it may specify a 100-
pound snow load in your area, but you want to build to
last forever and go for a 150-pound snow load. Or it may

not require a catch pan under a propane heating system, but for additional safety, you install one anyway. (Propane is heavier than air, and gas leaks tend to gather at a low level—a pan catches the leaking gas and vents it to the outside.) Sometimes you'll want to exceed the code.

You will need to get at least the following specific building permits for:

- The structure
- Roofing
- Plumbing and gas
- Electrical
- Mechanical (heating and air conditioning, including ducts)

You may need additional permits as necessitated by the type of construction you are doing.

What's the Procedure for Getting a Permit?

The procedure for getting a permit is relatively simple. You appear at the building department, with at least two sets of your plans, stamped with approvals from the homeowner's association (if any) and the planning department, and simply say you want a permit.

The counter clerk will usually determine what kinds of permits you need. After that's done, you'll be told a fee that you must pay (described below) and then you'll be told how long it will be before your plans are approved. Sometimes it's just a few days, but if the building department is large and busy, it could take up to a month. During that time your plans will be checked to be sure they are in compliance with the UBC and any local code upgrades.

Usually the building department wants at least some minor changes. It will call you in and show you them. If the changes are really minor, you can just OK them on the spot. Often, however, they require some redrawing of the plans and then a resubmission.

Once your plans are compliant, you'll be notified they have been approved and you can pick them up. When you do, you'll be given one set of plans stamped with building department approval. These must be kept on the job site at all times to be made available to the building inspector. A duplicate set of plans is kept by the building department.

What If There's a Problem With the Plan Check?

Unless your plans were professionally drawn (and even then), don't be surprised if you receive word that they require modification. I sometimes believe that the plan checkers don't really feel they're doing their job unless they can find at least one item needing modification in every set of plans.

Just be patient and make the changes required. If the changes conflict with something you want to do, you can call for a meeting at the building department between its engineers, your architect (if you have one), and yourself, where often a compromise can be hammered out.

On rare occasions, you may be turned down for a building permit. The building department will simply nix the whole idea. For example, you may be in a rural area where septic tanks are used. But there isn't enough room on your lot for a leach field. The building department says you can't build. You now have an unbuildable lot. (Reread Chapter 4.) Now it may be time to go back and have a heart-to-heart talk with the seller of the lot.

TRAP

As soon as you get a permit, information about the job is forwarded to the assessor's office. And when you complete the work, a notice of completion is likewise forwarded, at which time you can expect the tax assessor to raise your taxes based on an appraisal of the new home. It's unavoidable. You just have to grin and bear it.

What Do Building Permits Cost?

The price of building permits includes the cost of having someone check plans as well as the cost of having inspectors go out and check your construction at various stages. As a consequence the costs can be high. A thousand dollars for a complete set of permits for a home would not be unexpected.

What's much higher, however, are the building fees for schools and roads that many jurisdictions now tack on. These are based on the square footage of the home. Depending on the area, you could easily pay an additional $2000 to $5000 in such fees. It's something to consider when deciding to build.

Who Gets the Approvals and Permits?

It takes time to get approvals and permits. You may have to appear before a board of directors for your homeowners association. You may need to spend several hours or even days at the planning and/or building department.

If you have your GC or architect get the approvals and permits, expect him or her to charge you for the time spent. After all, it's work away from the job site for them. The cost could be substantial.

TIP

The building department will always ask for the name of your GC. If you're doing the work yourself, the building department may balk, saying that it would prefer a contractor do the work. However, I've never heard of a law that can prevent you from doing most work yourself. (Some counties may require that a pro do the electrical/plumbing.) But the building department may require that you sign a statement stating that you are residing in the property and will continue to live in the home yourself for at least 6 months. The residency requirement simply makes the assumption that you will do a good and safe job if you're going to inhabit the property.

Getting plans and permissions is a normal part of building your home. If you don't fight it, but just be patient and jump through the hoops, it should go quickly and easily.

9

Getting Accurate Bids

It's important to know the difference between a bid and a "guesstimate." A true bid is written down, and the contractor has to stand by it, whether it's too low or not. A guesstimate is an opinion of what something might cost. The contractor is not bound by it. If you get a guesstimate when you think you're getting a bid, you could be in big trouble.

This is not to say, however, that guesstimates don't have their place. When you're in the design stage of your home, you will want to have some idea of what things will cost. For example, should you put ceramic tile or granite on your kitchen countertops? A guesstimate will quickly tell you that the granite can cost up to four times the cost of the tile.

Or you may want to have a bay window extend out of your living room. A guesstimate will tell you how much extra that window is likely to cost. A guesstimate is extremely helpful when you play "what-if" games and when you make decisions early on. But accurate bids are what you must have once you get serious about construction.

In this chapter we'll look at both: first, how to get guesstimates and, then, how to get accurate bids.

Get "Ballpark" Bids from Contractors

Almost any contractor is willing to come out, talk to you, get a sense of what you're doing, and give you a verbal guesstimate. The only real question is, how accurate will the guesstimate be?

TIP

To get an accurate bid from a contractor, you need to have a set of plans and a list of specs, as well as a timetable for completion. If you don't have those, you're just getting a guesstimate.

Usually guesstimates by contractors will be high, because they will be figuring that you will not really know what you want and will change your requirements over time. The contractor has to build in protection in case you end up wanting something substantially different from what you are now asking for. Often contractors will give you a variety of guesstimates. For example, here's a typical contractor's guesstimate for building a home:

GUESSTIMATE FOR BUILDING A HOME

Shell—foundation, framing, skin, and roof	$60,000
Rough electrical and plumbing	$7,000
Drywall and insulation	$4,500
Finish electrical and plumbing	$13,000
Finishing (cabinets, doors, flooring, etc.)	$40,000
Guesstimate	$124,500

Note that the figures are for broad areas of construction. There are rarely details in guesstimates. And as noted, usually the guesstimates are high. Nevertheless, guesstimates are helpful to you in making your home building decisions.

How Do You Find Contractors to Give You Guesstimates?

If you're persistent, there's always someone who's willing to take the time to talk to you in the hopes that you'll eventually turn out to be a paying client. Just remember that the contractor is taking time out from a busy schedule to help you, so try to have your questions in order so you can be brief and to the point.

Check Out Materials Costs

Next, check with local building suppliers. If you had a small job, you'd probably check out a store like Home Depot. But for a whole house, you'll want to get a guesstimate from a supplier. The contractor can give you the names of several local supply houses.

Go to these places and get a feeling for what wood and other materials cost. Again, most of these places will want a spec sheet so they can do a "takeout" or firm bid for you. However, if you just chat with them, you can get a pretty good sense of what things will cost. For example, they may be able to give you a "whole-house package" guesstimate for framing. It may be off by several thousand dollars, but at least it will give you a sense of materials costs. And you can do the same with plumbing and electrical contractors and suppliers.

It's also not too early to begin looking at what finishing up the home will cost. Too often with construction, we get caught up in essentially the rough house: the foundation, framing, roofing, drywall, and so on. The real quality of the home, however, will tend to show in the cabinets we use, the appliances, the flooring, and so forth. It's a good idea to begin to get the costs for finishing up the home. You may be quite surprised to discover that the finishing will cost almost as much as all the rough work combined!

TIP

When you're looking at finished items, such as appliances or sinks, be sure you get all the extra costs. For example, a Kohler kitchen sink may cost $250. But, in addition, you will want a faucet assembly, which can cost another $150. And then there's the connecting pipes and materials, say, another $50. And with your sink you probably want a garbage disposal, say, another $75. Thus, your sink in reality, with extras, costs $525—and that's uninstalled. Get the real cost, not just the stripped-down cost without the necessary extras.

Add In an Allowance for Changes You'll Want to Make

Do you know exactly what you want done from start to finish, right now? If so, you'd be a remarkable builder. Most of us learn as we go, and as a consequence, we make changes along the way. In fact, changes are the rule rather than the exception.

Even though you may eventually get a plan and a series of specifications indicating exactly the materials you want, don't count on not changing your mind. Rather, as you begin work, you will undoubtedly decide that you want a window in a different location or a different toilet. Set aside an allowance for changes.

TRAP

As noted earlier, the most expensive costs are those involving changing a plan. It means the contractor has to do additional work, often involving removing work already completed. Since the changes aren't in the original bid, they may be added on a time-plus-materials basis, usually the costliest way to go. Keep your changes to a minimum and you'll save loads of money.

How much should you set aside for changes? It depends on how fickle you are. If you are always changing your mind and can never decide on what you want, then I'd set aside a hefty allowance, perhaps as much as 10 percent of the total costs or more!

On the other hand, if you're the sort of person who sticks by a decision once made, then you may want to add only 3 percent. This sort of person, once you've got a set of plans and specifications, won't want to change much.

TIP

You'll always find something you want to do differently. Unless you're very experienced, you won't be able to visualize how a project will turn out just from looking at the plans and specs. Rather, you will need to actually see the project being completed to know what it will look like. And inevitably you will find something you must have different. So even if you normally never change your mind, add in a small allowance for changes. You'll find you'll use it up.

How Do I Make a Go-Ahead Decision?

Once you get your guesstimates, you'll have some idea of what your home will cost. Now it's time to bite the bullet and make your "go" or "no-go" decision. Just remember, however, that you're still at the what-if stage. When you're just getting started, nothing's written in stone. You're just trying out different ideas, costs, and results to see how they feel. You can change things to make them work out. For example, in a home I was building, no matter how I tried to make it work, the costs were just too high. So I pared the home down from 2000 square feet to 1800 and made everything a little bit smaller. Suddenly, the figures all worked out!

Getting the Accurate Bid

The big reason for not getting accurate bids to begin with for most people is the cost. In order to get a contractor (or a sub) to give you a highly accurate bid, you have to supply a set of working plans and a highly detailed spec sheet. That costs money. When you're in the what-if stage, you're constantly making changes as you learn about costs and, indeed, about what you want and like. Hence, you got the guesstimates.

Now, however, it's a different story. You know what you want, and you've invested the time and money to come up with a set of plans and specs (see Chapter 8). Now you can get an accurate bid because you are able describe exactly the work you want performed.

Be Sure the Spec Sheet Is Detailed

Although we've glossed over it in various places in this book, the spec sheet, in some ways more than the plan, is the key to getting accurate bids. The spec sheet says what you want. It may take a builder or a supplier to determine how many board feet of lumber you'll need. But the spec sheet will detail the quality of that lumber. Similarly, it may take a builder to determine how many metal brackets you'll need, but the spec sheet will say whether they're to be Simpson or fabricated or whatever.

The specification sheet, when it's drawn up properly, will list all the types of items you'll need down to their size, shape, material, color, and manufacturer. From this sheet, anyone who is going to work for you, who is competent at his or her job, should be able to determine both the scope and the details of what you want. Consequently, when the spec sheet is added to the plans, you can get an extremely accurate bid.

Whom Should I Get to Bid?

You only want qualified people. That usually means GCs or subs whom you would be willing to have work for you. For example, if you know of a contractor in the area about whom people say, "Don't use him. His work isn't reliable," would you want him to give you a bid? Even if his bid were the lowest, would you want to accept it?

How Do I Handle Multiple Bids?

It's important to get at minimum three bids, and preferably five. I know that this involves a bit of hassle. It's so much easier to simply take the first bid, particularly if the contractor happens to be a really nice person. (Contractors and subs usually come across as really nice guys and gals because they know this will influence you to take their bids.)

But don't give in just because it seems easier. Spend the money to have extra sets of plans and specs made, and find at least three people to give you bids. Then you'll have a real means of comparison. And you could end up saving a bundle of money!

Remember, be sure that each person who bids does so on the same basis. Give each person a copy of the plans and the spec sheets. Be sure all the bidders know *everything* you want done. Then, when the bids come in, check them over to be sure they include all the work. It's really easy for a contractor to leave out some portion of what you want done and arrive at a surprisingly low bid. But when the job commences and the left-out portion is discovered, the bid suddenly jumps up there to what everyone else's was—or more.

TIP

Talk to the bidders. Make sure they understand *all* of what you want done. Make sure it's in writing as part of their bid.

Also, make sure all the bids are on the same basis. You don't want one bid to be for total cost while another is for time and materials. That's like trying to compare apples and oranges.

What If I Get Wildly Different Bids?

If the bids are all over the place, it means your plans, or more likely your specs, aren't clear and detailed enough. It means that the bidders really don't know what you want.

TRAP

You can always tell when your specs (or plans) are bad, because the bids will be all over the place, meaning that the bidders don't really know what you want (or that they are all incompetent, which isn't likely). When this happens, it's time to clarify your plans and specs.

What If the Price Is Too High?

It often happens that all the bids end up being higher than you were expecting. What do you do now?

You can always get a few more bids. However, if you already have three similar high bids, it's unlikely you'll get a quality contractor to come in for a lower one.

When bids are too high, my suggestion is to call each of the bidders and tell them your problem. Tell them what the bids were and that they're more than you want to pay or can afford. Sometimes, if one is more eager for work at the time, he or she may be willing to cut the bid a bit closer to what you want.

Should I Try Arguing a Contractor's Price Down?

You certainly can negotiate the price or terms of the contract with the contractor, as noted above. However, if you try to pressure the bidder to come up with a lower price, be prepared for stiff resistance. Most contractors have a really good idea of what their own costs are, and they have (or should have) learned early in their career the penalties for bidding a job too low.

Further, remember that the contractor does this all the time. You only do it occasionally (or perhaps only once). Most will have all sorts of arguments to prove that the price they are bidding is reasonable, if not a downright steal, and that the terms are thoroughly fair to all parties. Keep in mind that from their perspective, they may be right! You will need strong, reasonable arguments backed up by facts to change their minds.

TRAP

 Be wary of trying to knock a contractor's firm price down. Oftentimes, when contractors agree to a lower price, in their minds they are calculating that, yes, they'll charge you less, but they'll give you a lesser quality job, too. It's better to look for a different contractor who wants to charge less.

Should I Take a Low Bid?

As noted above, if you've done your homework—gotten a good spec sheet and set of plans—all the bids should be fairly close to each other. After all, the cost of materials is going to be roughly the same regardless of who does the work. And the cost of work is likewise going to be similar, unless someone is desperate and cuts you a real deal.

Which is why, occasionally, out of three bids, you'll get one that's way low. You'll wonder, should you take it, or does it indicate a contractor who's merely incompetent?

When I get a low bid, I first consider the bidder's references and background (from Chapters 6 and 7). Is the person a quality contractor? Does he or she have a good reputation?

If the person passes muster, then I always call the bidder and talk about the job. I make sure the person understands what's involved and that he or she, in fact, has bid on all the work, not just a portion.

Finally, if everything checks, I mention that the person's bid is lower than the others and wonder if there's a reason for this. You may find that the bidder has had a dry spell and is desperate for work. He or she, therefore, is willing to cut you a great deal.

If everything else checks out, I go for it, and so should you!

Once when I was taking bids on the foundation and framing of a whole house I was building, I had a contractor whose bid was nearly a third less than anyone else's. Yet he had the best reputation in the area. When I asked about the low bid, he said he was between jobs and he wanted to keep his crew working. If he could start work that week, he'd hold to his bid. Otherwise, he'd cancel it. I got him working right away, and he did a wonderful job.

Creating a Spec Sheet

Finally, let's talk about the spec sheet. If you buy a set of plans from a magazine or if you have an architect draw up a set of plans, you should be able to get the spec sheet for a few bucks more. However, if you're doing things on your own, you'll need to come up with your own spec sheet. It's not hard, but it does take some detail work.

When creating your spec sheet, be sure that you:

1. List everything you'll need for the job.
2. Be specific about size, shape, and quality. (For example, 16D galvanized nails.)
3. List appliances and prebuilt items by manufacturer and model number.

4. Indicate any special installation requirements and refer to drawings (for example, the living room radiant heater requires special venting as well as a gas line).

5. State that all items must meet building code standards in your area.

TIP

If you aren't sure of the exact item you want, you can include an allowance. For example, instead of listing a fiberglass shower-tub enclosure, give yourself a $400 allowance. You'll fill in the make and model later on.

TRAP

Be sure that the item you want can actually be purchased for the amount allowed. Sometimes a slight difference in shape or even color can make hundreds of dollars of difference in price. You'll have to come up with the difference. That's why it's better to check it out beforehand. (You're going to have to check it out sooner or later, anyhow.)

10
Cost-Cutting Ideas

Probably the most fun you'll have when building your own home will come from the design stage (that is, until it's all done and you walk through it the first time!). Here you can let your imagination soar and include all sorts of wonderful features, shot down only by your budget.

On the other hand, there are some ways to cut costs while you're actually building. In this chapter we're going to get a few tips about construction and costs that will influence both your design and your construction. In other words, here's a reality check.

TIP

Don't believe what people say about per-square-foot cost.

As you most assuredly know if you've looked around at all, construction costs are always given as so much per square foot. From the onset you'll be told that it will cost you $90 per square foot to build—or $125, or $200, or whatever happens to be the going rate in your area.

While this figure can be very helpful as a guesstimate, it's not always going to be accurate. For example, a few years ago I was building a home I had designed. I called up several builders asking for bids just for building the shell—the foundation, framing, sheathing, and roofing—not finishing off the building. Most builders really only wanted to know how many square feet were in the building. Yes, they went through the motions of giving me a written bid (detailed in Chapter 9), but in reality it was only a formality. They knew how much their bid was going to be the minute I told them the square footage. For example, one knew that she could do the foundation, framing, sheathing, and roofing for $55 a square foot (remember, we're not talking the entire construction cost here). The building was 2000 square feet, and so her bid came in right at $110,000. Most other bids were similar. Except for one old, cagey builder.

This builder actually looked over the plans in detail. He figured out how much wood it would take, how much roofing material, how much cement and steel for the foundation, how much for the sheathing. Then he calculated his labor costs. Finally, he added in his profits. It turned out he could do it for $45 a square foot, or $90,000. Whose bid do you think I took?

Per-square-foot cost is an average for all construction in your area. But your actual costs may be less (or more). In other words, if you don't build an average home, why should the average per-square-foot cost apply?

If you've carefully designed your home to cut costs, your actual per-square-foot cost can beat the average; it can be significantly lower.

TIP

Avoid corners and rounds.

You're on a budget, and you want to cut that square-foot cost down. Then put as few corners as possible into your building, and don't use any round areas.

But, you may protest, it's the angles and rounds that add distinction and character. True, but it's also the angles and rounds that add cost.

For every corner you want to build, it will cost more than to simply go straight. Every time you add a round turn, it has to be hand-built, and that adds far more costs. As a result, the cheapest building is going to be a rectangular box. The more you deviate from that, the more it will cost to build.

Does that mean that if you've got a tight budget, you're stuck with a box? Not at all. You can create an "ell" shape. You can add a facade.

You can put up dormers. A host of tricks can be used to transform and improve a bland boxy shape into something beautiful without adding so much to the cost.

However, it's when you zigzag the walls, create those round breakfast nooks, stagger the first and second floor, and so on that the costs add up. Keeping to the straight and narrow is simply a good rule of thumb. Violate this rule at your peril—the dollar signs are adding up every time you do.

TRAP

Don't make late changes.

I've said it elsewhere in this book, but it bears repeating: Don't start construction until you're completely finished and happy with the design!

Nothing adds more to the cost of constructing a home than late changes. What's a "late change"? It's when you've finished the design, have a set of plans, get going with the building, and then decide that you really don't want the kitchen next to the family room—you'd rather it be next to the living room. Or you'd prefer to have that bathroom ceiling 6 inches taller. Or you want a large bay window in the dining room instead of those small French windows. In other words, if you make *any change at all* after construction starts, it adds big bucks.

The problem comes about because the change often requires tearing out work that's already been done and then starting from scratch with new work. The more tearing out and reworking, the higher the cost.

Of course, some changes can be made without adding to cost, depending on where you are in the construction process. For example, you decide you want to change the location of some inside doors. If you do it during the framing stage, there's probably no extra cost at all. The carpenters simply put the door there instead of here. On the other hand, if the interior walls have already been drywalled, then you're going to have a charge. After all, someone has to rip out the drywall, rip out the existing walls, perhaps rip out some rough plumbing and electrical, and then redo it all, putting the doors where you want them. How much will that cost? Considering that reworking is often on a time-and-materials basis, it could cost twice as much as you paid for it to be done the first time!

TIP

Go up, not out.

It's cheaper to increase square footage by adding a second floor. After all, it only makes sense. For a second floor you don't need to build a separate foundation; you use the one you've got (although it may have to be made a bit heftier). You can also connect vertically to plumbing, electrical, and heating, so you don't have to run long distances horizontally with pipes and wires a second time. And there are other savings. So if you want to get more for your money, build a second floor instead of a bigger first floor.

TIP

Build in the winter.

Why build in the winter when the temperature outside may drop, when it could rain or snow? Simply because of the fact that the weather is inclement and most people don't build at that time.

Many contractors don't have work in the winter because of the weather. This is particularly true in climates where there is snow and heavy rain. If you can build during that time, builders will often cut you a deal on labor costs just to keep their crews working.

Similarly there is usually a cut in demand for lumber and other building supplies in winter. Hence, prices often drop, meaning you can save money on materials.

But, you may reasonably argue, how can I build a home in inclement weather? After all, there's a reason little building goes on then.

It's all in the planning. Start construction in the spring, finish it in the summer during the warm weather, and you've hit the peak of the building season (read "most costly").

On the other hand, start construction in the late fall, get your foundation in, frame and put up the roof and outside sheathing, and you can spend the winter finishing off the inside of the home, dry and relatively warm. You've missed the peak building season, missed the most costly time.

Some savvy builders look for a "winter house," a home built on a schedule as just described, so they can continue working during the inclement weather—and they usually price it accordingly. It's what smart builders do every year.

Note: In the Southwest the timing is reversed. Because of the superhot summers in some areas, you'll want to think about not building in winter, but doing it in summer.

TIP

Put in as short a driveway as possible

Driveways are expensive, whether you use cement, asphalt, or even just gravel. The longer the driveway, the greater the expense.

You may have a large lot, and you're wondering about where to place the garage. Place it near the street. Then you can have a narrow path leading to the home.

Yes, it will mean that you will have to carry your groceries further (and that may be a sufficiently important consideration that you'll want to place the garage closer to the house). However, you can literally save tens of thousands of dollars by shortening your driveway.

TIP

Dig as few trenches as possible.

Put all the utilities (or as many as your building department allows) in the *same* trench. This includes sewer and water and possibly electric and gas.

Digging trenches requires the hiring of a backhoe or, in some cases, a crew of laborers. The further you have to go and the deeper, the more expensive. If you can have just one trench instead of two or three, you can save a fair amount of money.

TIP

 If you don't have a lot of money to spend, then cut corners elsewhere, but spend it on the trim.

The trim is what makes the house look good—or bad. You can use moderate to inexpensive construction throughout, but if you then use high-quality trim, the house will appear to be of expensive construction.

Think of the trim as the clothes that make the person. The trim makes the house.

11
Getting Financing

Building your own home is a great idea, but how are you going to pay for it?

Unless you've got a bank full of money, you're going to need financing. And the time to start thinking about financing is before you even purchase your lot. Indeed, how you purchase the lot can determine the kind of financing you will need to get.

Financing the Lot

The traditional method of building your home was to go out and buy the lot for cash. Once you owned the lot free and clear, you'd go to a bank and get a construction loan. Since the value of the lot was typically about 20 percent of the value of the house and lot combined (when the building was completed), the lot served as your "down payment." In other words, you put up your equity in the lot, and the bank put up all the money needed to build the home.

In recent years, however, real estate has appreciated to the point where the land value is often as much as 30 to 50 percent of the value of the completed home and lot. In this case, it's impractical for most people to pay off the lot first. In other words, it's now become necessary for many people to finance the lot as well as the house.

STEPS IN FINANCING HOME CONSTRUCTION

1. Get the lot (including financing).
2. Get a set of plans.
3. Get a builder (or establish your credentials to build it yourself).
4. Get a construction loan.
5. Get a "takeout" or permanent loan.

Can I Get a Bank Loan for the Lot?

You can get a bank to lend you money to help you purchase a bare lot. But the bank won't want to do it unless you're a prime customer. And then the loan will typically only be for about half the value of the lot, at a high interest rate, for a short term.

TRAP

A big mistake to make is to think that it's as easy to finance a lot as a building. Not so. The hardest thing to finance in real estate is bare land.

Why are lots hard to finance? It's because lots are illiquid; in other words, they are hard to sell. If you don't make your payment on a house, the bank can foreclose and quickly find someone to buy the house. If you are delinquent on your lot payments and the bank forecloses, it could take 6 months, a year, or longer to dispose of the lot simply because there aren't that many people around looking for lots to build on. Hence, the bank discourages land loans by lowering the "loan to value" (LTV) and jacking up the terms.

TIP

If you need a bank loan to help buy a lot, ask for a combined personal and real estate loan. In this case you put up not only the lot as collateral, but your own good credit (as well as all your other assets!). Depending on your credit standing, you may be able to easily get enough financing to cover the entire lot cost.

Getting the Seller to Carry the Loan

Far and away the best lot financing will come from the sellers. As noted above, lots are generally hard to sell. To help facilitate their sale, sellers will very often be willing to carry back some of the financing.

For example, a lot may be for sale for $60,000. (I've chosen a figure for a typical lot in a choice area. While many lots cost less, keep in mind that in some areas of the country, the cost of lots begins at $200,000 and goes up from there!) Usually the sellers would love for you to come up with that whole amount in cash. But realistically, the sellers realize that it's going to be somewhat difficult to find someone with that much cash, so they instead agree to accept a third down ($20,000) and carry the balance ($40,000) themselves for a short while. In other words, they will be your lender. Now, you can get in with far less cash.

TIP

Some sellers, particularly those who are retired and need income, actually want to carry a mortgage. They reason that if they get the cash and put the money in the bank, they'll get a lower interest rate than if they offer you a lot loan. You may be able to arrange a long-term lot loan with them. Be sure, however, you get it subordinated. See below.

Typically they will want a reasonable interest rate, whatever the market warrants at the time. But they may also want a short term, say 2 to 5 years. What they are saying, in effect, is that they'll loan you enough money to get started. But you have to pay off their loan as soon as you put up your house. Indeed, they probably will want a clause written into their mortgage that specifies that it will be paid off as soon as you get your permanent loan.

TIP

It is possible to buy a lot for virtually nothing down, if you find a desperate seller. Some sellers will accept as little as $1000 and give you a mortgage for the balance. They simply want to sell, haven't been able to, and figure that as long as you make the payments, it's better than them having a lot that produces nothing.

Getting the Construction Loan

After you get the lot, the next step is the loan to handle the construction. As noted in Chapter 8, in order to get a construction loan you will need to have a set of plans and a builder (or be able to demonstrate your ability to construct the home). You will also need the following:

REQUIREMENTS FOR A CONSTRUCTION LOAN

1. Plans and specs
2. Builder
3. Good credit
4. Sufficient income to qualify for the loan
5. Equity in the property

Assuming that you have good credit (we'll get to this shortly), and a high enough income, the big stumbling block is often your equity. If you have the lot paid off in cash, this is no problem. If, however, you owe on the lot, it's a big problem. Before the lender will offer you financing, it will normally want that lot to be paid off. That means that you have two choices:

Pay off the lot from savings.

Roll the lot into some sort of overall financing.

The Loan and Your Credit Rating

There are essentially only two kinds of financing deals you can swing here. One works if you've got great credit, and the other works if you don't.

If You've Got Great Credit.   In this case, the lender says, "OK, you've got enough equity in the lot and your personal credit is sufficiently good enough that we'll cover you." Here the lender advances you enough money to pay off the lot loan and then lends you the money to build the home. Usually you will need to have at least enough equity in the lot to equal 20 percent of the combined value of the lot and built house. The lender may also require that the builder (or you) put up a bond to guarantee completion of the building.

If Your Credit Is Not So Great. On the other hand, if you can't swing the above loan, the remaining alternative is, once again, to have the sellers help with the financing. They can do this by agreeing to extend the term of the lot loan and to "subordinate" it.

Subordination means that the lot loan becomes subordinate, or secondary, to the construction loan and the takeout or permanent loan. (We'll get into permanent loans shortly.) For example, on our $60,000 lot, you get a $40,000 first mortgage. (It's "first" because it's the only loan on the lot.)

Without subordination, when you get a construction loan, that loan would become a "second." It's second because it was placed second in time after the lot loan. No lender, however, would agree to a construction loan in a secondary position.

With subordination, however, when you get a construction loan, that loan becomes "first." The lot loan automatically moves to second position. That's what subordination means—the lot loan is subordinate to the construction loan.

Some lenders will offer you a construction loan with a subordinate lot loan. The reason is that from the lender's perspective, with subordination the entire value of the lot is equivalent to equity. In any foreclosure sale, the lender gets all money realized before a dime goes to the lot loan (if, in fact, there's any money left over). Once again, however, a wary lender may require a bond to cover the construction loan.

TRAP

The best financing comes when you have a paid-off lot. When you have to finance both the lot and the construction of the building, you'll have to accept many financial compromises.

Note: Most lenders will require that any subordinated loan run for a long period of time, typically at least 10 to 15 years. This gives the lender confidence that you will have enough time to eventually pay off the loan, refinance, or sell the property.

What Is a Construction Loan?

We've bandied about the term "construction loan" without really defining it. So here's what it actually means. A construction loan is one in which you get partial payments of the loan as construction moves forward. For example, the total construction loan might be for $100,000. However, after you get the loan, no money is advanced to you until work begins. As soon as excavation and the foundation work is complete, you might get 10 percent of the money ($10,000). As soon as the framing of the walls is completed, another 10 percent ($10,000) is advanced. And so on until the home is completed.

There are advantages to both you and the lender in this system. From the lender's perspective, no money goes out until actual work has been done. This helps reduce the risk of advancing money on a home that never gets built.

From your perspective, you don't pay interest on the money until you get it. Thus, instead of paying interest on a $100,000 loan without actually having received the money, you pay only as the work moves forward and you receive the cash.

Drawbacks to a Construction Loan

There are some significant drawbacks to a construction loan.

DRAWBACKS

1. You lose some control. The bank says when the money will be doled out.

2. You have to find contractors who will wait to get paid.

3. The lender may disagree with you over what constitutes completed work, and so you may not be able to make timely payment.

4. The lender may significantly delay making timely payments because of its own internal bookkeeping system.

It's rare that construction loans move smoothly, although sometimes they do. When you have a lender and a contractor who are familiar with them, it can work well. If, however, one or the other is new to the process, you can expect difficulties and delays.

TIP

The best way to handle construction is to pay cash. This may be possible if you sell your previous home and then have the cash available to build. Of course, you will need to rent for a time, but many people overcome this problem by acquiring a trailer and living on the property during the construction period.

What Is a Takeout Loan?

No lender will give you a construction loan until you have a "takeout" loan commitment in place. A takeout loan is simply a conventional mortgage, a typical 30-year permanent loan. It takes out the construction loan—in other words, it replaces it. This only makes sense since the construction loan is short-term financing, just used until the home gets built.

You can get the takeout loan commitment from the same lender that gives you a construction loan. Or you can get it in the form of a firm commitment from another lender. Usually, it doesn't matter.

Where Do You Find a Construction Loan Lender?

While home mortgage lenders are everywhere, construction loan lenders are harder to find. Generally, most commercial banks should be able to handle a construction loan. However, some banks specialize in this kind of lending, while others are unfamiliar with it. You want a bank with experience in this arena.

TRAP

Beware of getting a construction loan from a "full-service" bank that doesn't have an operating branch near your lot. You'll need to be able to talk to the bank's rep on short notice about problems that crop up, and the rep will occasionally need to come out to the job site. All large banks offer construction loan financing, but the department may be in a distant city. Better to get financing from a smaller local bank that can cater to your needs.

First try the bank where you already have a relationship, where perhaps you have a checking or savings account. Then check the yellow pages under "Banks," "Construction Loans," and "Mortgages." Look for lenders who advertise that they handle construction loans.

When comparing different lenders, look for the following:

WHAT TO LOOK FOR IN A CONSTRUCTION LOAN LENDER

1. Experience—does the lender do these loans all the time?
2. Loan fees, charges, and interest rate—compare.
3. Does the lender insist you get its takeout loan?
4. The amount of paperwork it requires.
5. Does the lender require a bond?
6. What is the payment schedule like (how many steps)?
7. References (from satisfied customers).

Remember, you're the customer here, and the bank needs to satisfy your demands.

TIP

Never go "hat in hand" to a lender. The lender needs you every bit as much as (if not more than) you need the lender. It's strictly a business arrangement. If the lender doesn't satisfy your needs, look elsewhere.

What Kind of Permanent Financing Can You Get?

Just imagine that you're going out to purchase an already built home and need a mortgage. What kind of financing could you get for it? The answer is that there are literally hundreds of different loans available. (We'll look at several in a moment).

Your best bet, actually, is to begin with the lender who's offering you a construction loan. Assuming that lender also offers permanent loans (most do), see what kind of a deal the lender will make. Just keep in mind, however, that the deal may not be the best. And a takeout commitment from any other legitimate lender should do just as well.

Next check with a mortgage broker. This is an individual (or company) who specializes in home mortgages. He or she usually represents many dozens of lenders and can quickly send you in the direction of those who handle takeout financing.

TIP

Get "approved." In order to get most financing, you have to be approved by a lender. This process can take anywhere from a few days, if done electronically, to several weeks, if done the old-fashioned way by mail. It can be handled by your lender or mortgage broker.

It's important to understand that there are a few differences between applying for a takeout mortgage and applying for a mortgage on an already-built home. The most obvious is that in your case the home isn't there. That means that the lender must be willing to make a commitment (in writing) based on the estimated value of the home upon completion. Some lenders are hesitant to do this, but many find it no problem.

The lender will want to appraise the lot to see what it's worth. You will also need to submit a set of your plans. The lender will say it wants to analyze them, but it really only wants to see how many square feet the home will be and what type of construction (low-cost, moderate, or fancy) you're doing. The lender then multiplies the square footage by the appropriate average construction price per foot in your area and arrives at an estimated value. It will compare this amount with the price of surrounding homes, and if the estimated value is similar, the lender will give you a dollar figure based on the LTV (loan to value). For example, if the estimated value turns out to be $200,000 and the LTV is 90 percent, your maximum takeout loan would be $180,000. This will also be your maximum construction loan, since the takeout has to be enough to pay off the construction loan. (After the home is complete, a second appraisal will be made to confirm the value.)

TIP

Since the process of determining value is really guess-work, if you get a low initial appraisal, try a different lender. You might be pleasantly surprised at the different results.

Can I Get a Better LTV?

Yes, certainly. The baseline LTV is usually 80 percent. However, you can readily find permanent loans for 90 and even 95 percent. You will, however, need to have excellent credit to get these, or you may be charged a higher interest rate and you will need mortgage insurance (an extra $1/2$ percent). Again, your mortgage broker is your best source of increased financing here.

TIP

It's important to understand that the LTV is based on the final value of your home, lot, and you and building. That means that in most cases the takeout loan covers not only the construction loan, but also most of the cost of the lot.

Can I Pay Off My Lot Loan with My Permanent Loan?

Frequently you can. If you got the seller to carry back a subordinated second mortgage, there may be enough extra money (over and above what's necessary to pay off the construction loan) to pay off the lot loan. In fact, this is the very reason that many borrowers want the seller to carry back financing. Here's a typical example:

PAYING OFF YOUR LOT LOAN

Lot down payment	$20,000
Lot loan	$40,000
Construction loan	$150,000
Total value	$210,000
Permanent loan (90% of value)	$189,000
Your equity	$21,000

Notice that in the above example the permanent loan is almost exactly enough money to pay off the construction and lot loans.

Types of Permanent Loans

A host of loans are available to you. Here's a short list. (For a more detailed description, check out my book *Tips & Traps When Mortgage Hunting*, second edition, McGraw-Hill, New York, 1999.)

Fixed rate.   Available for a variety of terms, the rate and the payment do not fluctuate.

Balloon fixed.   This is a fixed-rate loan with payments based on a 30-year payback, yet with a balloon payment due at an earlier time, typically year 3, 5, 7, or 10. The advantage is that the lender will give you a lower interest than for a regular fixed rate. However, you must refinance when the balloon comes due, or sell.

Adjustable rate.   Here the interest rate and usually payments fluctuate according to market conditions. The advantage is that you get a much lower "teaser" rate to start.

Conforming.   The loan conforms to the underwriting guidelines of Fannie Mae and Freddie Mac. This is the lowest-rate loan you can get. However, the maximum loan is set, currently at $240,000.

Jumbo.   A loan for a higher amount than a conforming loan. Banks and other lenders will offer this as a separate mortgage or in combination with a conforming loan. The maximum amount is determined by each lender.

Hybrid.   Any combination of adjustable and fixed-rate loans. The different types of hybrids boggle the mind. There may be as many as a thousand on the market at any given time.

What About Credit Problems?

It's important to understand that building a house is not an alternative when you can't buy a house because of bad credit. You need good credit to buy a ready-built house, and you need even better credit to build one yourself.

That doesn't mean, however, that if you have some blemishes on your credit you can't get into a property. Quite the contrary. In today's market almost any credit risk can find financing, for a price. But the worse your credit, the higher the interest rate you are going to be charged.

TRAP

 Beware of companies that offer to "fix" your credit. The only way bad credit can be fixed is for you to establish a pattern of borrowing and timely repayment over a period of years. No credit-fixing companies can do away with true bad credit. It remains on your record for years.

To determine just what your credit actually is, check with the country's three leading credit bureaus (any lender you use will do the same thing!).

Mortgage Web Sites

Since Web sites change constantly, your best bet is to check out search engines with links to mortgage lenders. *Note:* While all offer takeout loans, you will probably have to contact them directly to determine if they offer construction loans.

SEARCH ENGINES

www.yahoo.com

www.excite.com

www.lycos.com

Search words that are helpful include

Mortgage

Home mortgage

Construction loan

HELPFUL WEB SITES

www.mortgage.com Mortgage broker with access to many lenders.

www.eloan.com Mortgage broker with probably the best and clearest lender and loan information online.

www.chase.com Chase Manhattan Mortgage, one of the country's leading banking lenders.

www.countrywide.com The largest independent mortgage banking lender in the country.

www.homefair.com An independent mortgage lender site. Offers school and city statistics as well as wizards to help you calculate your maximum mortgage.

www.quickenloan.com Quicken Mortgage from Intuit. A mortgage broker service. Its wizard calculator is one of the best I've tried. As of this writing, the site offers mortgages from six national lenders.

www.hud.com HUD, federal government Department of Housing and Urban Development. Contains loads of useful consumer information on housing. HUD does not offer mortgages.

www.fanniemae.com Fannie Mae, the country's largest secondary lender. You'll find all sorts of information on mortgages. (Much of it, unfortunately, tends to be highly technical.)

www.freddiemac.com Freddie Mac, the country's second largest secondary lender. Again, no loans directly to consumers, but filled with lots of useful information. (Also lots of technical information.)

Equifax	800-685-1111
Trans Union	800-916-8800
Experion	800-682-7654

Check with your mortgage broker for sources of financing if you have less than perfect credit. Many of the nation's largest lenders offer special programs, at a higher interest rate, for "B" borrowers.

Check out the lenders on the Internet. Almost all the country's major lenders have their own Web sites, and there are other sites that offer mortgage brokering.

Construction

12

Siting the House and Preparing the Lot

Finding the lot seems like the hard part, *until* after you've found it and it's suddenly time to site the house. Then, your first big building decision must be made: where to put the house? It's a vital decision.

The orientation of the house (where it sits on the lot) will determine if you take advantage of the lot's positives, or if you ignore them and end up with a house that is obviously awkwardly situated.

TRAP

A badly sited house sticks out like a sore thumb. Everyone who comes by realizes there is something wrong with it.

If this is the first time you've built, you may not realize the significance of siting the house. It may seem like just another of the many chores, and you may want to delegate the procedure to your contractor or to someone else. Don't. This is something *you* must do, else you may regret it ever after.

TRAP

Once the house is sited and staked and construction begins, you can't change the location. Even if you then realize you placed the home wrong, it's too late. You'd have to tear everything out, including the foundation, to make even a slight change.

While it is true that you can build a house that looks good on virtually any building site, the more exotic the site and the more radical the house required, the greater the cost. Ideally what you want to do is to work with the site to produce the best looking and most cost-efficient plan. In order to do this you should take into account the following factors.

Is There a View?

If there's a view, it normally takes precedence over all other factors. You will want to have the house facing the view. If the view is off the back of the lot, then you may want to flip-flop the plan, with the front of the house facing the back and the rear of the house facing the front of the lot. (The garage, of course, will always face the street.) Typically the main rooms (living room, family room, kitchen, and master bedroom) will be oriented to face the view.

Similarly, you may want to change your design in order to accommodate large windows on the view side. If you are restricted in the total square footage of window space allowed because of energy concerns, this means that rooms not on the view side will only have minimum-sized windows. This can also be a big factor in determining the type of heating you want and its location in the home.

TRAP

Nothing is worse than to get a set of premade plans and use them without modification to build a home on a view site. Inevitably the premade plans don't take advantage of the view, and you end up with a room such as the guest bedroom or even the back of the garage facing the view while the living room or master bedroom faces the non-view side. Be sure you modify any premade plans to take full advantage of the view the lot may have. (You often see this problem in tract homes.)

What Is the Relationship to Existing Homes?

You will want to site your home so that it blends in with existing homes. If your home is set further back from the street, or set further forward (as setbacks allow), or twisted at an angle (when all the other homes are perpendicular to the street), it will stand out and probably look like a sore thumb. Ideally your home will blend into its environment, and that includes fitting in with its neighbors.

Also, if all the other homes have a garage out front or a bold entrance or some other common denominator, it will look best if your house is similar. This doesn't mean that your home must conform to every feature of other nearby homes. It just means that it should not be playing a Sousa march while the other homes are waltzing.

What Is the Exposure to the Sun?

Some people insist on a warm southern exposure. Others want their homes to face west so they can see the sunset in the evenings, or east so they can be up with the sunrise. It depends on your tastes.

A lot also depends on the climate in your area. If you're in the northern part of the country where the summers are mild and the winters cold, you will probably want the side of your home with the most glass facing south. In winter the sun will tend to warm the glass and your home.

On the other hand, the opposite is true if you live in the desert or the Southwest. Here you have mild winters, but baking-hot summers. You will want the most glass facing north, where the shade of the house will keep the sun out in the summer.

What About Shielding from Bad Weather?

In most areas, one side of the home will get more weathering than another. This is because storms will typically sweep in from the same direction. While that direction may vary depending on where you live, it is usually from west to east and north to south. For that reason, the severe-weather sides of most homes are the north and west.

You can shield your home by placing the side with the fewest windows facing the harshest weather. Putting the garage in that direction also helps.

On the other hand, you may want to take advantage of the weather. For example, I once built a home on the crest of a hill that faced northwest looking down on a valley. Storms would sweep in across the valley and hit the northwest side of the home full on. However, that was a majestic view (far better than television!), and to take advantage of it, I placed most of the windows facing the inclement weather. Of course, they were double-pane glass and they had overhangs to protect them, and the walls on that side had extra diagonal bracing to handle the winds. Nevertheless, by going against the weather, the home gained in value.

Similarly, if you live in a hot climate, you may want windows facing the wind. It can help cool the home in the summer.

What About the Lay of the Land?

The easiest land to site a home on is perfectly flat. Few lots, however, are flat. Most have at least a gradual slope. If that's the case, you have to decide how the house will take advantage of (or work against) the slope.

For example, if the slope of the lot is down to the street, then the house will be higher than the street. This generally is considered a good position. Looking up at the house gives one a sense that it's bigger than it is.

On the other hand, some lots slant down away from the street. Driving up to the home, you'll look down on it. This perspective makes the house look smaller and tends to accentuate the roof. You may want to move the home slightly further back from the street or even angle it on the lot to defeat this downcast perspective.

TIP

Be sure to specify the height you want for the first floor. If the lot is on level ground, this shouldn't be a problem, as the builder will normally just match it up to the height of neighboring houses. But if your lot is sloped, it could be anybody's guess as to how high your first floor will be. If the builder puts it too low, you'll probably need extra costly excavation. Too high and you'll need to pay for extra foundation work to boost the height. Usually you'll want it about the midpoint of the slope that the house occupies, but not necessarily. Spend some time checking out the "look" of your lot to be sure.

A word about "cut and fill." If you're on a fairly steep slope, a contractor may suggest that the easiest way to develop a building site is to cut into the slope with a bulldozer about half the width of the house and then use the extracted dirt to fill an area down-slope to accommodate the remaining half width of the house. In this manner you use the existing dirt (and don't have to have it hauled away) and save excavation by not having to dig so far into the slope.

Be wary. Experience has shown that this cut-and-fill procedure can have disastrous consequences years down the road. The fill side can settle while the cut side remains stable. A house built half and half, therefore, can literally split down the middle, with one side sinking (on the fill) and the other side remaining high (the cut side). I actually saw one instance of this happen.

It's better to cut far enough into the hillside so that the entire house is on the cut. Or remove enough dirt so that the entire house is on the fill. Of course, be sure that the fill has been properly tamped down to reduce settling.

What About Water Flow?

In a typical lot, water will drain from the rear to the front and then out to the street and the usual storm drains. Of course, if you have a very large lot or if it slopes to the rear or side, the water will not run toward the front.

The advantage of having the water run to the front is that it moves from your private yard to the public street. If the water runs to the back or sides, it usually moves from your lot onto someone else's lot. And similarly, someone else's water moves onto your lot.

While I know of no legal consequences that may accrue from the natural flow of water, if you attempt to change the flow over your lot so that it adversely affects a neighbor, that's a different story. The neighbor, with good reason, may strongly object and even take you to court to get relief. All of which is to say that you should pay special attention to the flow of water off the lot.

A separate issue is how the water will lie once the house is built. A friend once owned a house that was set in a sort of hollow on its lot. Whenever it rained, the house tended to be in the middle of a giant puddle. My friend had to put in an expensive drainage system, including a sump pump, just to keep the ground under his home dry.

Ideally, you would build the home on a high spot on the land so that water would flow away from it on all sides. If you're on a slope, be sure that the water can flow around both sides of the house and down the slope. If there's an area on one side where the water is blocked, think about including drainage as part of your building scheme.

TIP

If the soil has a lot of clay and drains poorly, it is usually a good idea to place a special drain pipe (called a "French drain") near the periphery of the house. This is a pipe with holes spaced every few inches or so in it. It is covered with gravel on all sides as well as felt paper (to keep dirt from clogging it) and has a slope that allows the water that fills it to run out. The drain keeps water away from the foundation of the home.

Finally, there's the matter of erosion. It's worth your while to take a few moments to sit back and examine the lot before you do any excavation. Are there signs of erosion? Will the placement of your house be in the path of the erosion? Is there a way you can situate the house that will avoid the eroding area or even reduce it? A bit of careful consideration here can save a lot of problems later on.

Where Will Your Septic System Go?

In Chapter 5 when we talked about a buildable lot, we described watching out for different types of soil. The hope is that you had it tested before you bought, so that now you know you can accommodate a leach field (if you're putting in a septic system) and that the soil will support your home (or that you'll need a special foundation.)

Now you need to plot out exactly where the leach field will go. (Be sure that you have the county's sanitation engineer approve your plans.) The last thing you want to do is to build your home only to discover that part of it is where the leach field must be!

TRAP

Don't put in the leach field *after* you excavate and start building the home. Put it in *first* so you'll know where it goes and will be able to site your home accordingly.

The septic tank works by allowing anaerobic bacteria to "digest" the waste. Nevertheless, some solid waste will accumulate on the bottom of the tank. Typically this must be removed every few years (depending on the usage of the home's septic system). It's important to locate the tank near a driveway so a pumping truck can get to it. It's also important to have a removable cover on the tank and to make sure the tank is easily identifiable and accessible.

What About Ingress and Egress?

You have to get to your home. How will you do it? Is there a natural place for the driveway? What about the path leading to your door?

TRAP

Avoid long driveways. They cost more to put in and are more difficult to maintain, and when they have to be replaced, they will cost you a small fortune.

Ideally you won't want a short, straight driveway and path, because it tends to look abrupt and, well, cheap. What you want, while still relatively short, is a driveway with a curve (if possible) and a curving path to your door.

TIP

If you must place your home close to the street, zigzagging the path leading to the door will offset an otherwise too symmetrical look and make the appearance more pleasant.

What About Hooking Up the Utilities?

Ideally, the utilities will be available up to the edge of your lot. For work purposes you will want to set up a temporary work pole at the building site and put in a temporary circuit breaker panel with a couple of plugs. That's so the workers have electricity to operate their power tools. Have a professional do this.

Our concern here, however, is getting the utilities such as sewer, electric, gas, and water to your building site. These normally will be underground, with the possible exception of the electric service. (In most areas, electric service to new lots is underground as well.)

Be sure to plan the route of the utilities across the property. Be wary of dragging them across any easements that your lot may have. An easement is a grant, such as a right of way, to someone else such as a utility company. Frequently lots have utility easements along one side. If you put your utility lines across an easement and later on the utility company needs to cut through for its own purposes, it will cut right through your utility lines, and because you gave the easement, it will be up to you to pay for having them replaced!

You also want to avoid any leach field, driveway, or garage. If you put the utility lines under any of these and there's a problem years later, you'll have to dig up the leach field, driveway or garage floor to get to the lines!

TIP

When bringing in both water and sewer lines, save money by using the same trench. Be sure it is deep enough to accommodate the "drop" required for the sewer to the street. Be sure the water line is significantly above the sewer line, so that if there is a double break (as can be caused by an earthquake, tree root removal, or later excavation), there is less likelihood of contamination of potable water. Usually the sewer line is placed to one side of the water line so that if later repair is required, you don't have to break through the water line to get to the sewer line.

Note: Depending on the building code in your area, you may or may not be able to bring the electric and gas lines through the same trench as water and sewer.

What About Landscaping?

Most people don't think about landscaping until after their home is built. That's a mistake, because then it's too late to take advantage of some natural features of the lot that may otherwise be excavated away.

For example, preserve trees. Trees take ages to grow. If you have mature trees on your lot, try to work your home placement around them. Some people even go so far as to build their homes around the trees rather than remove them.

TIP

When the builder grades the lot, he or she will undoubtedly remove the topsoil. Be sure to specify that you want this soil set aside and not hauled away, as may be the case for subsoil, boulders, gravel, or whatever else is found. The reason is that later on you can have this valuable topsoil put back on the ground. This way you won't have to pay extra for landscaping soil when you're finished building.

Further, if you take landscaping into account when you lay out the lot, you can set aside children's play areas, and you can define areas where you want trees to help block out unsightly vistas or even create borders between your lot and your neighbor's. A living wall of bushes or trees can sometimes be far prettier than a fence. Just be sure that you don't violate HOA restrictions or CC&Rs regarding the height of living walls.

Finally, if you are building on a slope, you may want to begin planting ground cover immediately after the lot has been graded. The sooner the cover is in, the less chance there will be for erosion.

TRAP

Don't plant anything until you have a sure source of water for irrigation. Otherwise what you plant may quickly die, and you will have wasted your money and effort.

Staking the House Site

Once you've considered all the factors indicated above, the next step is to meet with your GC and stake the lot. You should stake out both the leach field (if you need one) and the exact location of the home.

You should first indicate on the plot plan exactly where the home will go. Take into account easements, setbacks, leach fields, and so on. Then, you should go to the lot and, using the plot as a guide, put in the stakes indicating where the house will go.

You should also measure from the edge of the home to the lot line (as indicated by your surveyor's stakes or flags) to be sure that you've observed all the necessary setbacks. You don't want the building inspector coming by after you've poured your foundation and telling you it's a foot too close to your neighbor's house!

The front building line is probably the most important since if you don't observe the minimum setback requirement, it could mean that later on you'd have to tear out the foundation. Stake it carefully. Then stake out the side building lines, again being sure to observe the necessary setback requirements.

Whom Will I Get to Grade the Lot?

If you have a contractor, he or she will get someone with a tractor to come in to do the grading work. If you're your own contractor, use the techniques discussed in Chapter 7 to locate an excavation company.

Be sure that the excavator understands where you want the house located and exactly the grades you want. You should have a plot plan giving heights. These people are experienced and can often come within inches of exactly the correct elevations.

Also, be sure to specify whether you want the dirt excavated to be hauled away or saved. And identify specific problems, such as large boulders that might have to be blasted. (Blasting can cost as much as all the rest of the excavation combined, or even more!)

13

Building a Strong Foundation

Build a strong foundation and your house will stand forever (or at least until someone decides to knock it down!). Build a weak foundation and you'll spend much of your time fixing cracks in walls, floors, and ceilings which crop up as the foundation shifts and breaks. I always try to build foundations stronger than the minimums that the building code demands.

While you can build the foundation yourself, unless you've done this sort of work before, I suggest that at least the first time you hire a sub to do it. Concrete masons are contractors who specialize in foundation work. There are also footing subs who specialize in doing grading, excavating, and putting in the footings (described below).

If you do it yourself, it's important that you understand two things about foundations. First, the work is very heavy. Concrete is not for those with weak backs.

Second, excavating the correct-size hole, determining that the ground underneath is sufficiently solid, building the bracing wall, installing the rebars, and getting the right mix of plasticizers (hardening chemicals) in the concrete are tasks that require knowledge and experience. So at the least hire someone to coach you along the way.

TRAP

Don't think you can learn everything you need to know about foundations from a book, this one or any other. You need to have the experience of seeing it done at least a couple of times before you can get the hang of it.

What Is a Foundation?

The foundation actually consists of two parts: the footing, which rests on undisturbed soil, and the foundation wall itself, which rests on top of the footing. Often the foundation wall and footing are a continuous pour of concrete.

The purpose of the footing is twofold. Its primary function is to spread the weight of the home over enough soil that the house will be easily supported. Too small a footing and the weight of the house could cause sinking and cracking. The second function is to provide a rigid platform on which the foundation itself can be constructed.

Note: While footing and foundation normally run around the entire periphery of the home, you may have footings placed at various points under the home as a base for supporting posts.

How Deep Should the Footings Go?

In clay and other expansive soils, deep (18 inches to 2 feet) and wide (16 inches to 2 feet) footings may be required. On packed gravel, much smaller footings may be needed. The size of the footings will also be determined by the weight that's to go above them. A two-story home will require bigger footings than a single story. Be sure to check with your local building department. If the soil in the area is a problem, the building department will know about it and will insist on specifying the depth and width of the footings.

TRAP

The footing should always extend below the frost line, the maximum depth to which the ground freezes in winter. If placed above the frost line, soil expansion from freezing can lift and crack the footing—and the foundation.

I always prefer to go several inches wider and deeper than the minimums required by the building department. Yes, concrete is expensive, but a few more yards poured in this critical area will be reflected later on in a house that doesn't crack or shift.

Do I Need Extra-Heavy Footings in Some Areas?

Yes, if there is extra weight to support. For example, I once built a home where the entire center of the roof was supported by three posts with a heavy beam running across them. The footings for those posts had to be far larger than the peripheral footings. How large is determined by an engineer who will calculate the load and determine the footing size.

If the house is going to have a masonry chimney, it's also going to require a special footing (because of the weight). Be sure to determine the size and location of the chimney footing at the time the rest of your concrete is poured.

Should I Use Steel?

Concrete is very strong. However, it is subject to cracking. Steel rebars (reinforcement bars) reduce the possibility of cracking substantially. Further, if cracks should occur, the rebars will hold the foundation in place. Today most building departments (but not all) require rebars as a matter of course in building footings and a foundation.

Generally speaking, you will have rebars running both horizontally and vertically in a foundation. The horizontal rebars run the entire length of the footing. If it's a peripheral footing, this means all around the house.

TIP

The more rebars, the better. If the code requires two, put in three. For even more strength you can run a continuous cable around the entire periphery of the house.

What About Building on Slopes?

Often the foundation and footings are not level because the house is built on a slope. If that's the case, then the footings must follow the lay of the land. However, the strongest way to build the foundation (basement walls) is to make them in steps. Without steps the foundation wall can end up being very tall on the downside of the slope. Unless its thickness is increased to accommodate its height, the wall will be relatively weak at the bottom.

It's important when making steps in a foundation to be sure to make the foundation sufficiently thick to withstand any side pressure (for example, from snow) and to insert vertical rebars for added strength.

How High Should the Foundation Be?

That depends on the plans for your home. If you're going to have a crawl space, the foundation should normally be 18 inches above grade. On the other hand, if you're going to have a slab, the foundation may be no higher than the slab itself or (depending on local code) 6 to 8 inches above the slab. If you are going to have a basement or are building on a slope, the height can be as much as 6 to 8 feet.

Should I Use Concrete Blocks?

You can save money when building a foundation by using prepoured concrete blocks. They are available these days in a relatively small variety of shapes. All have hollow areas in their core cut out to save on material. (Concrete blocks that are solid core are generally referred to as "concrete bricks.")

Concrete blocks are also preferred by contractors because you don't have to build the foundation all at once. You can build part of the foundation, then go do something else, and come back later and continue on. With poured concrete it must be done all at once. Further, with concrete blocks you don't have to build forms.

It's important to understand that concrete blocks are not as strong as poured concrete. However, you can increase their strength in two ways. First, when building a wall of concrete blocks, you can increase the strength by running rebars vertically through the blocks and placing wire mesh or rewire (reinforcement wire) horizontally between layers. Also, you can fill all hollow areas with concrete.

TIP

A wall of concrete blocks is not as strong as a wall of poured and reinforced concrete. However, a wall of blocks with rebar and concrete in the hollows is much stronger than just a wall of naked blocks.

What About Slabs?

A concrete slab is poured as a floor in many parts of the country, particularly the Southwest. The slab is poured right on top of the ground, so there is no basement or crawl space. Often plumbing and vents are laid right in the slab. In some construction, heating vents and pipes are laid into the slab when it is poured.

TRAP

While it may seem obvious, be sure your foundation (and slab) is level. Leveling can be assured by building the forms correctly and using lines to check for height at all corner and centers. Yet sometimes contractors fail to do this. If the foundation is off, you'll have to use shims under the sill plate to level the house. Extensive shimming can weaken the structure. If the slab is off, everything in the house will always be on a slant, not a particularly desirable result.

It's important to understand that the slab is not usually part of the foundation. Rather, the footings and foundation wall are first poured. Then, the slab is poured in the center.

In some cases, however, the slab "floats." In this construction the slab and the footings and any foundation walls are poured at the same time. (Figure 13-1.)

If you or your contractor are not familiar with floating slabs, I suggest you do not try them. I've seen them attempted by those who are inexperienced with them with disastrous results.

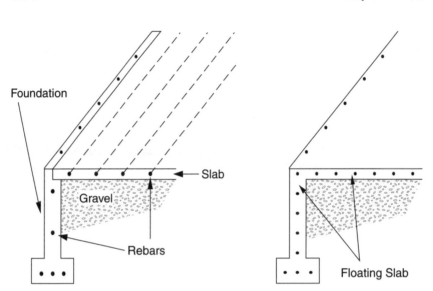

Figure 13-1. Slab and Foundation

TIP

Be sure that you use crisscrossing rebar in the slab. A slab without rebar will crack. Also, add an extra inch to the thickness of the slab, particularly at the edges, over and above the minimum the building code requires. You'll be well pleased when your slab doesn't crack.

Have Your Poured Concrete Tested

Be sure the contractor uses good concrete. It should end up with a hardness of 2800 pounds per square inch or more.

The concrete can be weakened or strengthened by the amount of water and plasticizers added. Builders often want to add more moisture because it makes the concrete workable for a longer time. This, however, also weakens it.

The ASTM (American Society for Testing and Materials) specifies certain tests for concrete. For testing, you take samples (they are taken in what looks like gallon coffee cans) at various locations at the time the concrete is poured. The samples are allowed to harden.

Then, after a certain amount of time, usually 2 weeks, they are smashed in a hydraulic press. If the concrete has the required resistance, it passes the test. If it fails the test, it is tested again after 21 and 28 days. (No further hardening occurs after 28 days.)

If the concrete still fails the test, the foundation has failed. Typically the building department will require you to tear it out and start over. That's why using good concrete at the onset is so important.

Use Enough Anchor Bolts

The frame of the house is anchored to the concrete through the use of heavy "J" bolt anchors (usually 10 inches × ½ inch). These are inserted into the concrete when it is still wet. The threaded end of the bolt extends above the top of the concrete, and the sill plate is then bolted to it. (Figure 13-2.)

The purpose of anchor bolts is to keep the house from slipping off the foundation in high winds, earthquakes, or other movements. Years ago, these bolts were not used. That's the reason that in the Loma Prieta earthquake in San Francisco, so many older homes slipped off their foundations. These homes are now being retrofitted.

Typically these bolts are spaced every 3 or 4 feet. However, they can be spaced as close as 1 or 2 feet. The only additional expense is usually the extra bolts.

TIP

For $50 in extra bolts, you can virtually double the stability of your home and cut in half the chances of slippage off the foundation. Just place the bolts closer together.

I once built a home where the concrete masons didn't read the plans carefully and put the anchor bolts in every 3 feet, although the plans called for them every 18 inches. When the building inspector noticed the error, he closed down construction. The solution required that additional anchor bolts be drilled into the foundation at the appropriate intervals, a very expensive proposition.

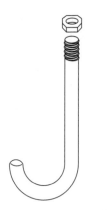

Figure 13-2. "J" Bolt Anchor

TRAP

Almost inevitably, after the foundation wall is poured, you will discover that some access hole was not left open. The opening for the water or sewer pipes or the drain for the heater might have been forgotten (or purposely not taken into account). A hole will have to be made through the concrete. Be sure the hole is *drilled.* An easier method is to use an impact hammer to make the hole, but this will crack your foundation. Use the more costly and time-consuming drilling approach. It may be more difficult at the time, but your foundation will last longer.

Waterproof the Foundation

If the foundation is against soil where there is heavy water content (but not stagnant water requiring a French drain), applying a moisture barrier (usually drain tiles and/or an asphalt coating) will help keep basements and subfloor areas dry. This should be applied to the exterior of the finished foundation after the forms have been removed and before the excavation is filled in.

Beware of Using Stone Foundations

Some homes, particularly very expensive ones, use stone walls. In this case, the temptation is to use stone for the foundation as well.

However, using stone, whether rubble or cut stone, is extremely expensive, and the result is not nearly as strong as poured, reinforced concrete.

One solution is to use concrete for the footings and then stone for the foundation. This compromise can result in a stronger house. A much better solution, although more costly, is to simply put in a conventional concrete foundation and then just use stone for the facing.

Don't Use Wood Foundations

Wood foundations were once the standard. A wood foundation begins with a mudsill, usually a redwood or pressure-treated board, laid right on top of a mud-gravel base. This is the typical kind of construction used prior to 1920 in many areas of the country. Even if allowed by building code today, however, it is the weakest foundation and the most likely to slip. It should be avoided. (Figure 13-3.)

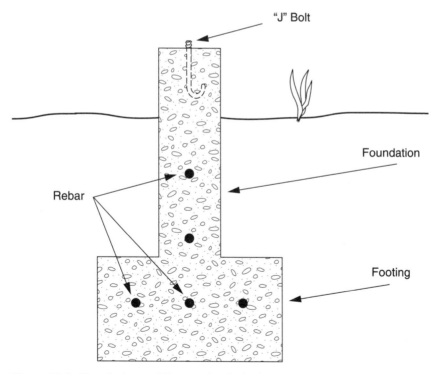

Figure 13-3. Foundation and Footing for Staked Home

14

Framing and Sheathing

The framing and installation of windows makes for dramatic progress. You could have watched for a month or more as the excavation, the septic system, and the foundation were poured. At the end of that time, your home may not have looked like much more than some grubbing in the ground. But once the framing starts, the house seems to leap up. In a very short while, what is discernible as a home is standing.

While you may relegate the framing and windows to a competent carpenter crew, it's important that, at the least, you understand what's happening. You will want to make some decisions concerning how the framing is handled.

Installing the Bottom Plates

The first step in framing is to install the sills. You'll recall from the last chapter that when preparing the foundation, bolts were embedded in the concrete and then extended upward. The idea is to now attach boards (usually 10-foot 2 × 6s) to the top of the concrete foundation and hold them in place by the bolts. This is where the wood meets the cement (Figure 14-1.).

Usually a layer of felt or some insulating material is placed between the concrete and the sill plate. This evens out the concrete and provides some insulation. Holes are drilled in the wood plate to accommodate the bolts, and then washers and nuts are used to lock the plate down.

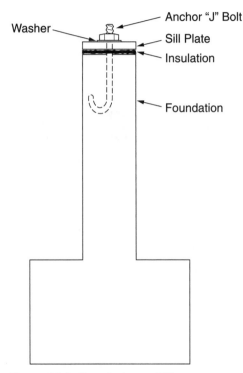

Figure 14-1. Foundation to Sill

TRAP

It's important that the bolts be placed at minimum distances from each other, typically no more than 2 or 3 feet (as specified by your plans or the building department). If the bolts are spaced further, the entire frame will be more prone to shifting from wind or earthquake.

Putting In the Floor Joists

The floor joists are laid on top of the sills. In a relatively narrow room, the joists may go right across from one side of the peripheral foundation to the other. However, in most homes that are fairly wide, the joists will have to be supported along their run by piers and girders.

Remember those extra footings that were poured in the various locations in the center of the foundation area? Now wood posts are attached to them, and girders (beams) are laid across. They supply the additional support for the floor joists. (*Note:* Footings may not have been placed for the cement piers. Rather, depending on the quality of the ground, the piers may simply be laid in a shallow hole. Be sure to follow your building department's requirements here.) (Figure 14-2.)

TRAP

Sometimes contractors will simply use a wood cap on top of the cement footing and nail the post onto it. Some building departments will allow this. However, a structurally superior method is to embed a steel plate into the concrete footing with metal braces sticking out. The post can then be bolted to the steel. When raised slightly above the concrete, this metal also provides a termite barrier.

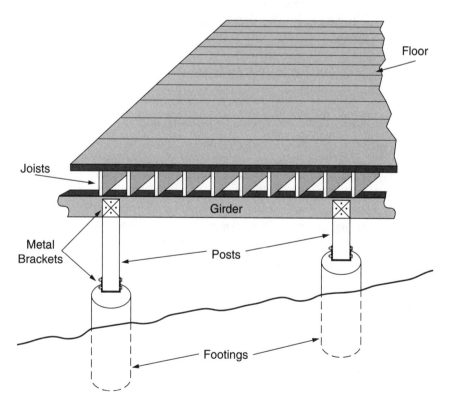

Figure 14-2. Floor Foundation

Usually the posts are wood (although they may be steel), anywhere from a minimum of 4 × 4 to much greater thickness, depending on the weight they must support. The engineering you do on your plans will specify the thickness of these posts, as well as the beams, the joists, and the maximum length these can extend.

You may want more than the minimums. The big problem with floors is that if they aren't built hefty enough, they tend to sag. By using thicker joists and shorter runs, you beef up the floor.

TIP

One of the big problems with floors is that they tend to squeak when you walk over them. One method of avoiding this problem is to glue the subfloor directly to the joists, so it won't have any give and, consequently, won't squeak. But this is only partially effective, since over time the joists will tend to give slightly, the flooring will separate, and squeaking will occur. A better solution is to use the manufactured "I" joists now available. These are high-tech joists composed of a composite material providing great strength in a form that does not give. Though more expensive than conventional wood joists, they tend to greatly diminish squeaking.

To finish off the joists, a floor header is usually placed around the periphery, and solid blocking is inserted. A floor header is simply a board placed at the ends of the joists where they lie on the foundation sill. Solid blocking consists of boards cut the same height as the joists and laid between them so they cannot twist or slip. Sometimes bridges (metal or woods pieces) are placed diagonally between the joists to stabilize them (to keep them from warping). (Figure 14-3.)

TIP

I personally don't believe that bridging helps in any way, yet some contractors swear by it. Unfortunately, it's time-consuming and difficult to construct. If your con-

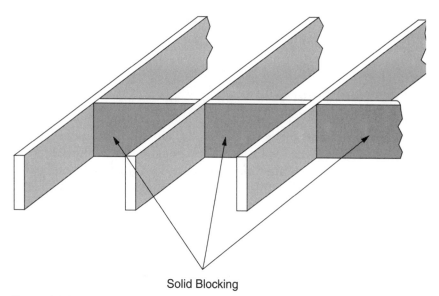

Solid Blocking

Figure 14-3. Solid Blocking

tractor wants bridging (or if your building department insists on it), see if your contractor (or building department) will accept the simpler solid blocking method.

Building a Short Wall

If your land is flat and your peripheral foundation runs all around the house and is level, you needn't read any further. However, if the foundation is at different levels, you will need to build short walls in spots to reach from the foundation to the floor. These shorts walls are called "cripples."

Part of the reason for the name is that these short wall pieces are not as strong as the regular walls. That is because they typically lack diagonal bracing.

TIP

Be sure to add diagonal bracing to all short walls. This is most easily done by nailing a piece of $5/8$-inch (minimum) plywood every 3 inches on studs for the entire wall. The effect will be to make the wall as strong as if not stronger than the rest of the home.

Building the Floor

The subfloor goes right on top of the joists. As noted, it is often glued as well as nailed. The type of subflooring varies, depending on the construction used. Typically an inexpensive grade of plywood is used, often ³/₄-inch. Sometimes a compressed-wood particleboard flooring is laid on top of the plywood for additional strength. (The plywood has great holding strength, while the particleboard's stiffness keeps the floor sturdy.)

There is another type of construction that relies on a "floating" subfloor. Here thicker 1¹/₂-inch interlocking plywood squares are used. A series of piers is placed every 4 to 6 feet to support the plywood. This floating-pier foundation is used where the ground expands and contracts greatly over the seasons, for example, in places where the soil is clay and there are winter rains. The floor actually moves up and down slightly, accommodating the changes in the ground.

The finish floor (hardwood, carpet, tile, etc.) goes right on top of the subfloor, but usually is not laid until the rest of the framing is done and in some cases (as with carpeting) until the rest of the home is finished.

Special Treatment for Bathrooms and Kitchens

If you're going to have tile in the bathroom and/or kitchen, you will need to treat the flooring there specially. The most common method of handling this is to use a special tile subfloor made of compressed wood laid directly onto the plywood subfloor. This is screwed and glued to the subfloor and then sealed to provide a smooth surface for tiling.

A better choice is to lay a bed of cement. The best bed for tile is cement, since it can be leveled precisely. To accomplish this, tar paper or some other impervious material is laid on the subfloor, and then a layer of concrete is poured. Wire mesh can be added to the concrete for strength. The tile can then be adhered to the concrete.

Building the Garage Floor

The garage floor is usually laid right on top of the ground (actually on top of a bed of gravel and an impermeable membrane) in the form of a concrete slab. However, in some construction sites where the home is on a steep hill, the garage floor will actually be supported off the ground by a foundation wall and be built of wood. There's nothing wrong with this, as long as the proper engineering has been done to ensure that the garage floor can withstand the weight of several cars.

Building the Walls

There are many different methods for framing. However, in truth, only one method is widely used, the platform frame. Here, the walls for each floor are put up on each deck. In other words, the home is built one floor at a time, a series of platforms.

A variation of this is the "balloon frame," where the wall studs reach from the deck of the bottom floor continuously to the top of the second (or third) floor. After the bottom deck is built, the next floor is "suspended" above it. This requires the use of scaffolding and is a more expensive type of construction. On the other hand, the continuous wall studs from the bottom floor to the top of the top floor provide greater stability.

Steel post construction involves embedding steel posts in the concrete at the corners of the home with laminated wood beams extended across them. In this type of construction the walls are more or less filled in and do not support the ceiling.

Wood post construction is less common because of the cost of the wood these days. (Steel, unbelievably, is rapidly become competitive with wood!) Here wood posts are attached to the footings by means of steel caps and then run the height of the home. Sometimes additional wood beams are placed horizontally between them. The post and the beams provide the basic structural support for the roof. The exterior walls in this type of construction are basically nothing more than partitions. Wood post construction typically leaves the wood exposed, presenting a pleasant, natural look.

Wall framing itself consists of vertical studs placed every 16 inches or so apart. In some areas of the Midwest to save on construction costs, a greater width between the studs, sometimes 24 or even 36 inches, has been allowed. Be wary of this type of construction, as it seriously compromises the wall. It will have little resistance to wind or shaking. A minimum of 16 inches between studs should be used. In some very hefty construction, the width is only 12 inches.

TIP

Be sure that diagonal bracing is installed. This comes in three forms. A metal brace can be laid across the outside of the studs diagonally from floor to ceiling and then nailed on each stud. Or a plank of wood, typically a 1 × 6, can be cut into each stud diagonally. Or a sheer wall of plywood can be placed flat against the studs and nailed every 4 to 6 inches. The diagonal bracing keeps the wall from collapsing sideways and is an important and integral part of construction. There should be diagonal bracing on every outside wall repeated for the length of the wall.

A double top plate (two pieces of wood) goes on top of the studs. The next floor is built on top of it. Particular concern must be taken at the corners, which require extra support. The basic method of handling this is to have the double top plates overlap and to box in posts built of studs. The diagonal braces can be cut into the boxes for additional support. In areas where there is concern about earthquakes or heavy winds, additional metal bracing should be used at the corners.

Building the Interior Partitions

Usually the exterior walls bear the weight of the roof. The interior walls in most cases are simply partitions. The exception is when a central interior wall supports a roof beam.

The partitions are built in much the same way as the exterior walls. A bottom and a top plate have studs located between them. As with the outside walls, the studs should be no more than 16 inches apart. Often entire partitions are constructed on the deck and then lifted into place.

While the exterior walls are often built with 2 × 6 materials, to save costs the interior walls are often built with only 2 × 4s. This, unfortunately, has the consequence of making the walls shallow, more easily transmitting noise from room to room.

Building in Soundproofing

While the very nature of the exterior wall (thick, with sheathing and insulation) makes it relatively soundproof, not so with inside walls. They are rarely insulated and are usually simply 2 × 4s onto which wallboard has been nailed. As result, they are not much more than sound transmitters.

Since you are building this home for yourself, it will be worth your money to spend a couple of extra bucks to build soundproofing into the interior walls, especially between the bedrooms and the rest of the home. The cost is only as much as it takes for additional studs and insulation, probably not more than a couple of hundred dollars for the entire house.

TRAP

Many contractors simply don't know about or don't want to bother with sound insulation. You'll have to insist on it to get it.

The basic way to insulate the interior walls is to create a baffle that keeps the sound from being transmitted through the wall. If you nail pieces of drywall onto both sides of a stud, the sound on one side is transmitted through the drywall via the nails into the stud and out the other side via the nails and drywall.

The solution is to build two walls, one for each side. For example, use a 2 × 6 top and bottom plate and then double the number of 2 × 4 studs and stagger them on the plate. (See Figure 14-4.) The result is that each side of the wall has its own studs. Sound cannot easily be transmitted across them.

Sound can still, however, be transmitted across the airspace in the wallboard. To stop this, you will need to fill the space with insulation. Common fiberglass insulation will do nicely. In the process most of the sound across the barrier will be eliminated.

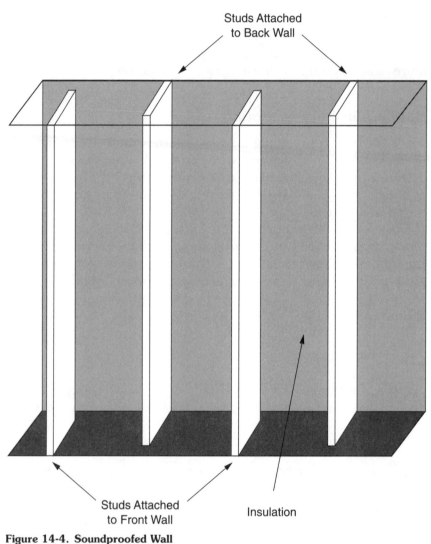

Studs Attached to Back Wall

Studs Attached to Front Wall

Insulation

Figure 14-4. Soundproofed Wall

Building the Window and Door Openings

Windows and doors need to be indicated on the deck so that they can be built as part of the framing. The construction of the frame for these is relatively simple, but important. Double studs are used, with the inside stud used to support a "header." A header is a heavy piece of wood that goes across the top. It distributes the weight of the roof or floor above, so that there is no sagging over the door or window. If you've ever been told that in an earthquake the safest place to stand is in a doorway, it's because of the heavy header located above.

The size of the header is determined by the span. Your plan engineering should specify all header sizes. Don't be surprised by the heftiness of the beams used.

On windows, the bottom of the framed-in window is called the "sill." On doors and windows, the stud that supports the header is called the "trimmer." On wide spans, double trimmers may be needed.

TRAP

Be sure that fire blocks are inserted between studs. These are pieces of wood the same size as the stud, cut to fit and placed about halfway between floor and ceiling. If there's a fire, they prevent it from moving upward in the wall to the roof or the next floor.

Be sure that any spaces created when framing, such as boxed-in corners, are insulated. Without insulation they could allow drafts or cold spots to occur in the house.

Putting in Shower Stalls and Bathtubs

Very likely you'll have at least one bathtub and two shower stalls. The quality you choose will help determine how finished your home looks. However, whatever you choose, there's a basic logistical problem that must be attended to. Premade shower stalls and the bathtubs are typically too big to fit through the doorways to the house and bathroom. Therefore, they should be installed before the interior framing is complete.

TRAP

Don't forget the tub and shower enclosures. If you wait until after you have the framing done, you'll end up ripping out walls to get them in!

It goes without saying that the rough plumbing should also be done as soon as the foundation is completed and before the floors and framing are finished. We'll have more to say about that in Chapter 16, on rough plumbing and electrical.

Installing the Windows and Exterior Doors

Once the framing and (sometimes) the sheathing are complete (including the framing of the roof, discussed next), the windows and exterior doors are installed. It is hoped that these will fit neatly into the openings left for them. The windows are nailed onto the frames from the outside.

When installing windows especially, it's important that they be squared in their frame. Of course, it should go without saying that all the construction should be squared. However, even with the best of intentions, the window framing will be off one way or another. Shims made of small pieces of wood that look like shingles can be used to square up the windows.

If the house is wrapped, be sure the wrapping is cut to fit snugly against the windows, lest drafts be let into the house. The doors are nailed onto their frames using shims to get them placed square. We'll have more to say about doors and windows in Chapter 17.

Building the Staircase

Any home that has a basement or second floor is going to have a staircase and often a landing halfway up. This is usually constructed on site.

The basic support of the stair comes from two boards at the edges (and sometimes a third in the middle) running the length of the stairwell. These are called "stringers," and they are notched to accommodate the steps.

The width and height of the stair will vary depending on the height of the stairwell and the space available. Usually the building department will specify minimums. The steps are then simply nailed down onto the stringers.

Pay particular attention to how the stringers are attached top and bottom. Usually the bottom of the stringer simply rests on the deck with a thrust block (a wooden block inserted at the base of the stringer to keep it from slipping forward). At the top it leans flush against the joist with a bearing board underneath to keep it from slipping down. The top may also be attached using metal straps and the bottom affixed by having the stringer laid flush against the floor joist with a bearing board underneath to keep it from slipping. Note that the stringers are not simply held in place top and bottom by nails. Rather, boards are inserted to give direct support.

Installing the Sheathing

The exterior sheathing is the last to be installed. It is typically plywood, and in some cases it forms the exterior wall of the home. In other cases, it is simply the base, with bricks, stone, shingles, or other wall materials installed on top of it.

If the sheathing is not the final wall exterior, then it typically will be some form of pressed-wood particleboard. It's important to use the right materials. Particleboard will not hold nails as well as plywood does. In any kind of stress situation the particleboard will tear and the nail hole will get bigger, while the plywood will remain undamaged for far longer. As a consequence, if you're going to use particleboard, it should be nailed far more closely than plywood. Often the nailing schedule for particleboard is twice as close as for plywood (every 6 inches, for example, on studs instead of 12 inches, every 3 inches at the end instead of 6 inches). One big reason for using particleboard is because plywood has become so expensive. If you use it, however, be sure you use it properly.

Exterior Wall Coverings

You have a wide choice of what to put on the outside of your house. My personal favorites are 5/8-inch plywood, which has grooves in it and simulates vertical paneling, and stucco, both of which I have used.

You can, however, use any of the following:

DIFFERENT KINDS OF EXTERIOR WALL COVERINGS

Stucco. Actually portland cement that's first sprayed and then troweled on as if it were plaster. It's put on in several coats (scratch coat is first, brown coat is second) over wire mesh (and a tar paper barrier), and the last coat (the color coat) actually has the color you want mixed into it. Obviously, it requires no additional painting. The advantage of stucco is that you can get a variety of finishes (determined by the plasterer) and that the coating is solid and thick (typically ¾ inch or more) and encases the entire house. The biggest problem is cracking over time.

Plywood siding. This comes in 4 × 8-, 4 × 10-, and 4 × 12-foot sizes. When nailed according to a schedule that puts nails in every 4 to 6 inches on studs, it adds enormous strength and diagonal bracing to the house. It will last almost indefinitely, but it must be painted immediately to keep the wood from deteriorating. Be sure that exterior-grade plywood is used. It comes in a variety of woods and designs.

Metal siding. This got a bad rap a few years ago, but if installed properly, it can last almost forever and seldom needs painting. Great care must be taken to see that no moisture is allowed to get behind the siding, else mold and mildew will eventually destroy the wall.

Wood planks. These are typically of cedar, pine, or redwood, although any hardwood will look attractive. The planks are nailed onto the exterior of the house with a vapor barrier behind them. The boards are typically tongue and groove or applied with a batten over the edges. The big reason these are not frequently used is because of the great cost.

Shingles. Shingles, essentially roofing shingles, can be used as wall covering. Care must be taken, however, to see that they are affixed in such a way as not to come loose and fall off.

Masonry. Brick and stone give a quality look to a home, particularly if they are used sparingly for accent. Usually the exterior wall is fully constructed with plywood sheathing before the brick or stone is added. As with hard woods, the cost is usually the prohibiting factor.

Earthquake and Wind Bracing

In areas where the ground moves or there are strong winds, additional bracing is often required. Probably the most effective method is to attach the corners of the house to the foundation by steel.

Essentially what this involves is using bolts to secure metal hooks in the foundation at all the corners of the home. Then steel rods are run up to the top plate of the wall where they are fastened. In this way the wall is directly and solidly attached to the foundation. Any movement up and down will not break the wall apart and separate it from the foundation.

As an additional precaution, a metal brace can be run across the top of the top plate all around the house and attached to the supports that run down at the corners to the foundation. In this way it is almost impossible for the walls to come loose.

Of course, there is the matter of the roof. Metal clips attaching the roof rafters to the wall's top plate will make sure the roof won't go anywhere. Similar clips holding the rafters to the central ridge beam secure the house completely. By this method, even if all the shingles of the roof blow away, the basic framing should remain.

15
Roofing

A roof needs to meet three criteria:

1. It should be pleasing to look at.
2. It must not leak.
3. It should be able to withstand the elements, including wind and snow.

The type of roof you use will depend on all three criteria. In some areas of the Southwest you may find that a flat, or deck, roof works well. However, in the northern states where there is ample snowfall, a flat roof would quickly collapse.

Further, the appearance of the roof should blend in with the types of housing that are nearby as well as the lay of the land. You don't want to use a gambrel roof in an urban setting, although it would fit right into a rural lot.

The Types of Roofs

There are essentially just seven types of roofs (Figure 15-1):

The deck roof. This roof is simply flat. It is found in areas where little roof load is required. Often it is finished off with a coating of tar onto which white gravel is thrown. It is one of the least expensive roofs to build, although the maintenance over the years can be heavy.

The shed roof. This looks exactly what it sounds like. It is the basic roof found in lean-tos or sheds. However, depending on the lay of the land, it can be very effective when there is a view on only

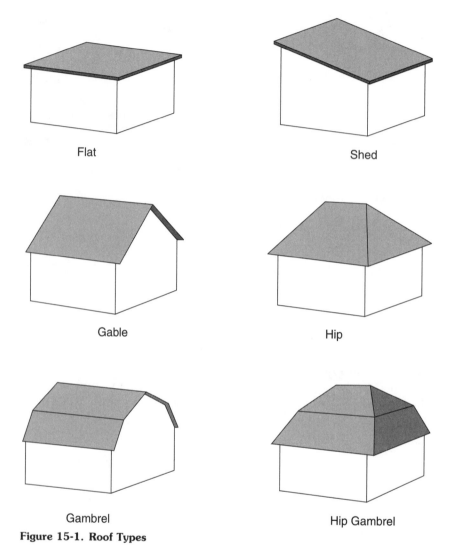

Flat

Shed

Gable

Hip

Gambrel

Hip Gambrel

Figure 15-1. Roof Types

one side of the house. It allows that side to have taller windows and greater view exposure.

The A-frame. Here the roof and the walls are all built as one. Actually the A-frame is a gable roof without a house built under it! A-frames have been popular as inexpensive mountain homes. However, the very design limits the available space inside. Most of these types of homes are smaller in size.

The gable. This is probably the most popular roof style. Usually it is symmetrical, with both sides being of equal slope and length. It's supported by a ridge beam and the walls at the sides.

TIP

I recently built a home that used a modified gable design (Figure 15-2). One side was only half as long as the other, and the pitch on the short side was shallower, allowing for second-floor windows on that side instead of dormers.

The hip roof. This is like the gable except that the ridge beam is shorter with a separate slope at the sides. This is the most common design found on tract homes. When building in areas where there is snow load, this home is also popular because of its strength.

The gambrel roof. Here the gable roof is modified by having two different slopes. The angle is thus reduced, which means that there will be additional attic space inside. Adding dormers further increases the inside space. This often gives the appearance of a large country barn.

The hip gambrel. Yet another variation on the gable. It has hips on all four sides. I have seen this roof used on some Southwest

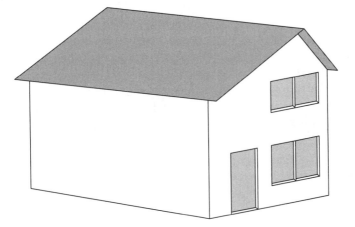

Figure 15-2. Modified Gable

homes, where it is attractive because of its striking difference from most of the other nearby roofs.

Judging the Roof Pitch

One of the most important considerations with a roof is its slope or pitch. Besides the appearance it gives, the pitch also contributes to the strength of the roof. For example, in areas of the country where there is heavy snow, a steeply pitched roof need not be built nearly as hefty as a flatter roof because the angle contributes to the strength.

Roof pitch is generally expressed as a ratio—the amount of rise over the run (or width). For example, a roof that rises 5 inches for every foot would be a 5-to-12 or 5/12 roof.

The Roof Load

Generally speaking, roofs have two different kinds of loads. Snow loads are referred to as "dead" weight. The snow simply bears down, drawn by gravity. On the other hand, wind produces a lateral load as it pushes on the roof. In some instances there is even an uplifting load where the wind gets under the eaves and tries to raise the roof.

The way the roof distributes the loads to the walls is an integral part of the home's construction. For example, a gable roof that does not have an independently supported ridge beam (where the beam is supported by posts going all the way down to the foundation) would tend to push outward on the bearing walls under a heavy load, thus collapsing the house. In order to avoid this, there must be a lateral support at the base of the roof and across the top of the walls. Similarly a strong lateral force (wind) against a gable roof that is properly supported for weight load will tend to push against the opposite wall, again putting additional stress on the house. A hip roof will add the strength necessary to avoid this problem.

When submitting your plans to a building department, you will be told that the roofs in your area must conform to minimum dead and lateral loads. For example, in warmer climates, a dead load of 40 pounds per square foot may be allowed. In areas where it snows, however, a snow load of 100 pounds or even 150 pounds per square foot may be required.

TIP

All roofs must be engineered to withstand the anticipated loads in the area.

Constructing the Roof

The type of materials used in the construction of the roof will have to be part of its engineering. For example, in the Southwest it is common to use masonry tiles on the roof. However, the downward pressure of these tiles is so great that unless the roof is properly engineered, it will collapse of its own weight.

TRAP

Be wary when buying roofing materials. Remember that the roof has to be able to withstand the weight of the materials themselves in addition to the necessary load.

There are basically just two ways to build a roof: one stick at a time and a manufactured truss.

Stick-Built Roofs

Here the roof is built "one stick at a time." It is constructed on site by carpenters. It has several basic components (Figure 15-3):

Rafters. These are the boards that lead from the walls up to the ridge.

Ridge board. The ridge board is what creates the peak.

Collar beams. These keep the roof from spreading apart and collapsing the house.

Ceiling joists.   They support the ceiling below as well as keep the roof from spreading apart.

A variation on the gable stick-built roof is to have bearing posts supporting a heavy ridge beam. Here the weight of the roof is taken up by the posts, and only a portion is distributed to the walls. Therefore, the pressure to collapse the walls by putting pressure outward is eliminated. The post-ridge roof, thus, allows you to have an open attic and or a tall ceiling. The other peak-roof types can be modified in a similar fashion to create a large open area.

TRAP

Stick-building a gable roof with posts supporting a heavy ridge beam is much more costly than other types of roof construction. However, the wide-open feel it creates inside is often well worth the expense. (Figure 15-4.)

The stick-built roof is relatively easy to construct. However, take care in using it when you want to create an ell or a turn in the roof. This requires creating a valley, which, if improperly constructed, can leak.

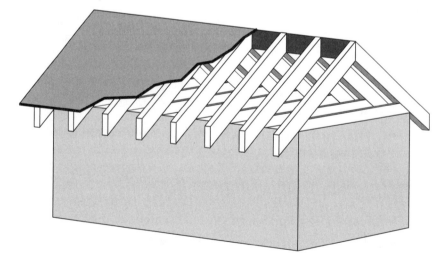

Figure 15-3. Stick-Built Roof

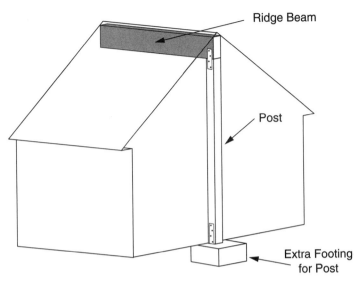

Figure 15-4. Gable and Post

Truss Roofs

A truss roof is essentially a roof that has been engineered and designed for maximum load and minimum weight and size and is built in a factory. To create it, engineers put all your load factors into a computer, along with the dimensions of your home, and the computer program spits out a series of designs. These designs are built in a plant to rigid specifications, and then the entire truss is carted to your home site. A typical truss will use only a fraction of the wood compared with a stick-built rafter, beam-and-joist construction. (Figure 15-5.)

There are many pluses and a few minuses  to truss construction:

PLUSES

1. The roof can be put up in a single day. Once the trusses are constructed and hauled to the site, it's simply a matter of a crane lifting them into place while carpenters nail them down.

2. You don't usually need interior bearing walls. In other words, none of the partitions needs to support the weight of the roof. All the weight is supported by the exterior walls.

3. Because the junctures in trusses are built with plywood or steel connectors, they supply the same strength as much larger pieces of wood that are stick-built.

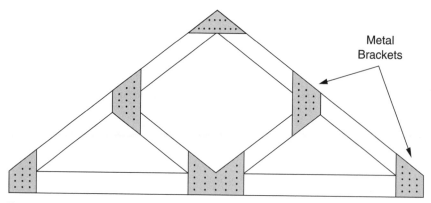

Metal
Brackets

Figure 15-5. Manufactured Truss

4. Although trusses are expensive because of the engineering and factory construction involved, overall they usually end up being cheaper than stick-building the roof on site.

MINUSES

1. You need a truss-building factory nearby. If you have to haul the trusses long distances, you can lose their financial advantage in hauling fees.

2. The truss eats up the attic space. You will find it difficult (but not impossible) to have high ceilings with trusses.

TIP

Work with the truss builder. I wanted a room above a garage I was building. At first the truss builder said it couldn't be done. However, with patience, a "hole" was made in the center of the truss to accommodate the room. Similar things can be done to create the effect of a high ceiling. (Figure 15-6.)

Sheathing the Roof

Once you have your roof up, you have to cover it. The most common covering is plywood sheathing, at least ⅝-inch thick. (Be sure to use exterior-glued plywood—typically it's rated CDX, with the C mean-

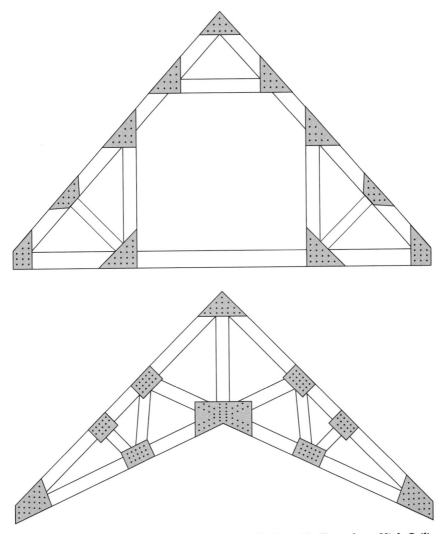

Figure 15-6. Manufactured Truss with a Room Built Inside/Truss for a High Ceiling

ing a finished surface, the D a rough surface, and the X exterior glue.) The plywood is cut to fit and then nailed according to a strict nailing schedule. The plywood provides support for the roofing materials as well as offering overall strength to the roof.

If you are going to use wood shingles, another method is preferred. It is to nail boards on the roof at regular intervals (with at least 3 or 4 inches between them). Roofing paper is placed on the boards and then shingles on top of that. The advantage of the board method is that any moisture getting underneath the shingles is allowed to evaporate through the spaces between the boards into the attic. This prevents the wood shingles from getting soggy and producing mildew and mold.

Roofing paper or "felt" is placed beneath most roofing applications. In the case of tile roofs, it is the roofing paper that keeps much of the water out. It performs much the same function with wood shingles. Properly applied fiberglass/tar shingles, on the other hand, can themselves provide an impermeable barrier.

A variety of products can be applied to valleys and the edges of roofs. The most common contains a sticky surface on one side and affixes itself to the roof as soon as it is laid down. It provides a much more impervious surface than simply roofing felt.

Roof Coverings

Today there are a wide assortment of different roofing materials that can be used. Here's a partial list:

ROOFING MATERIALS

Wood shingles. Used much less than other kinds both because they pose a fire hazard and because they are increasing in cost. The heavier shingles are called "shakes."

Ceramic tiles. Will last almost forever, but are expensive and heavy.

Asphalt shingles. Will last about 15 to 25 years, are heavy, but are relatively inexpensive. New three-dimensional types are quite attractive and are now widely available.

Fiberglass shingles. Look like asphalt, but have a higher flame retardancy. These are recommended in areas where there is a high fire danger.

TIP

Asphalt and fiberglass shingles come in a self-sealing version. Here the bottom edge has a glued area. Heat activates the glue, attaching the top shingle to the one below it. The biggest problem is that the glue area is typically covered by a thin layer of protective plastic that must be removed. Careless roofers don't remove the plastic, and, hence, the effect is lost. Be sure to ask your roofer about this.

Cement shingles.   Come in a variety of shapes and sizes, are somewhat lighter than ceramics, and are less expensive.

Metal.   Available in sheets and in shingles. Can be made in almost any color. Older versions tended to rust through. Modern versions are anodized and last almost forever. The biggest problem is that they dent, so that if a branch falls on the roof, it can leave a noticeable mark.

Flashing

Flashing is applied in valleys, around chimneys, at vents, at wall intersections, and near gutters. It is usually made of aluminum or galvanized steel. In the old days, lead was hammered and used as flashing, but in most places this hasn't been done for years. Usually flashing is fabricated on the spot to meet specific roofing needs.

The application of flashing is most important. It should be done by an expert, because it needs to go underneath layers of roofing material in such a way as to prevent any water from getting through.

Ventilation

Finally, there is the matter of ventilation. This is one of the most important parts of building a good roof, and yet it is often given the least attention.

All roofs will accumulate a certain amount of moisture. It comes with changing temperatures and weather conditions. The question is not whether you can avoid moisture, but rather how you can control it. The answer is adequate ventilation.

Most roofs with attics can handle the ventilation problem through the installation of vents. If you look up at a typical gable roof, you'll see a vent at either end. The idea is that the air will pass from one end of the home through the attic to the other, drying out the roof

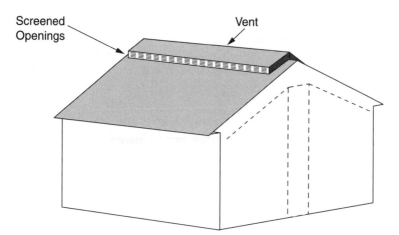

Figure 15-7. Ridge Vent for Roof Without an Attic

and the attic space. Typically these are boxlike devices with a grill-work as well as a mesh to prevent bugs and birds from getting into the attic.

The size and the number of vents depend on the amount of attic space and roof area. You don't need a lot of vents or big ones, but you do need to have some.

TRAP

Builders sometimes pay too little attention to attic ven-tilation. In summer the temperature in an attic can reach 150 degrees or hotter. Adequate venting will drop the temperature. Building in a fan with an auto-matic thermostat to turn it on at a high temperature is also a good idea and costs only around $35 a fan if done when the building is under construction.

If the roof has no attic (the roof is on one side of the rafter and the interior ceiling on the other), adequate ventilation can be pro-vided by drilling air holes in the solid blocking at the bottom and using a ridge vent at the top. (Figure 15-7.)

16

Electrical and Plumbing

Plumbing and electrical tend to be the costliest to hire out. Yet, in my opinion, they are the easiest for the homeowner to do, IF you know how.

The reason is threefold: First, there's little heavy lifting. You aren't going to be struggling with heavy timbers or wallboard.

TRAP

 CAUTION! Don't attempt to do electrical or plumbing (particularly gas) work yourself, unless you are experienced and competent in this area. The consequences of improperly installed wiring, fixtures, or other such work can be dire. ALWAYS have a professional supervise your work. Don't rely on a building inspector alone to check it out. It goes without saying that you should never work on the electrical circuits unless the power is off! Don't try to save money here by letting an incompetent (yourself!) do the work; always hire a professional if you can't do professional quality work yourself.

Second, designing the systems is logical, and you can learn almost all that you need to know about design from books readily available on the subject. The only really hard design is with wastewater, and that's because of the venting necessary—and again, you should be able to learn how to do it from books.

Finally, the assembly usually involves soldering, gluing, and screwing, all of which you can easily learn, if you don't already know how. (Many Home Depot stores, for example, offer courses in gluing plastic pipe and soldering copper pipe.)

All of which is to say that you can save a bundle of money doing the electrical and plumbing yourself, if you know how. On the other hand, if you don't, you can at least participate in the design. Just be sure to have everything checked by a professional.

Rough versus Finish Plumbing

The plumbing (as well as the heating and air conditioning) is done in two separate stages. The first is called the "rough." In the rough stage, which occurs partly during the pouring of the foundation and partly during the framing, the plumbing lines are run. Some may have to be poked through walls in the foundation; others set in a concrete slab. The basic drain system is put into place with toilet, sink, shower, and other drains and water supplies put in as soon as the decking and framing are done (or as necessary along the way).

The second stage occurs after the drywall is in and the home building is almost completed. At that point the finish work occurs. This includes setting the toilet seats (usually after the flooring is in place), installing sinks and faucets, and hooking up to the potable and wastewater systems.

Mechanical work, which involves ductwork for the furnace and air conditioning system as well as vents, is also done in two similar stages. Rough occurs during framing, while finish occurs after the house is largely completed.

Hooking Up to Your Water Supply

You should have already dragged the water supply from the street to the edge of your home. Now it's a matter of poking a hole through the foundation wall to bring it under the house. I prefer creating the hole at the time the concrete is poured. However, that's usually inconvenient. The preferred method by most contractors is to use an impact hammer to drive a hole through for the lines. It is hoped that you've thought ahead and brought the line in at a spot convenient to getting into the home.

TRAP

Usually holes in concrete are driven through using an impact hammer. Contractors like doing it this way because it gets the job done quickly. The problem is that this frequently cracks the concrete. A better method (for the homeowner) is to *drill* through the concrete. This, however, is laborious. You have to decide what's more important, a quick job or one that's done right.

It's more problematic if you are using a well. You will want to locate the well as close as possible to the home, for ease in pumping. Care must be taken, however, since if you're using a well, chances are you are also using a septic system. The well must be far enough away from the septic system that wastewater does not contaminate the well water. The county sanitation engineer will usually specify the minimum distances. If possible, you might want to spread things out even further. (A lot depends on the soil and how well it absorbs water.)

TRAP

Don't assume that just because you've followed all the steps, the well water is pure. Have it tested initially and then at regular intervals. Most states provide a strict testing regimen that looks for fecal material as well as trace amounts of poisonous metals and compounds. Testing can be costly, but it's worth it.

Assembling the Rough Plumbing

You should have a plumbing plan. It will specify the types of pipe you will use, their rough location, and the way everything will be vented. Most building departments will want to approve these plans.

Of course, once you're on the job site, things change. However, the general plan should still be followed. In particular, with potable water you want to be sure that you're using the right size and type of pipe, that it is located and supported well (so it can't easily be damaged), and that it comes up through the floor in the right places!

Dealing with Wastewater

Similarly, with wastewater there are varying sizes of pipe you must use for toilet, sink, shower, and tub drains. For example, usually a tub drain need only be 1½ inches in diameter. But a shower drain must be 2 inches. A toilet, on the other hand, requires a 4-inch drain. Only so many drains can be connected together, and everything must be vented. Get a book, as noted above, that will give you the values for each drain (the drains are assigned numbers) and how and where to assemble them.

TRAP

 Be sure to include many clean-outs. These are capped openings in the drain system that let you access it when (not if!) the line gets plugged.

Gravity is how most wastewater systems work. All the drain pipes must have sufficient pitch so that both the gray water and solid refuse will flow through them. You want to be sure that you don't have any valleys in the pipes where puddling can occur. This could be a potential health hazard.

Venting is necessary to allow for free flow of wastewater and avoid unpleasant sewer gases from entering the house. It is accomplished by having a wet trap at the bottom of every drain. Enough water is captured in the trap to fill the pipe, and so fumes cannot pass. Of course, the only way for the water to be captured in the trap is if there is a vent to the outside air. If the pipe were a sealed system, siphoning would suck the water out of the trap, allowing the gases to get by.

Testing the Wastewater System

Proving out a wastewater system is an experience that everyone should encounter at least once in a lifetime. It occurs after the entire system has been hooked up. The drain system is plugged at all its openings, and a water hose is put in place at the lowest vent on the roof. Water is then pumped into the entire system. An alternative is to plug the system and fill it with air under pressure. This, however, is often harder to do at a job site.

This results in enormous pressure, particularly if the house is two or three stories tall. Any bad fittings will result in immediate leakage. Usually you must hold the water in the line until the plumbing inspector comes by to see there are no leaks and approve it.

TRAP

Be careful when you drain the line. Don't simply open the bottom plug all at once. The first time I did this, I got drenched! The amount of water contained in a wastewater system is enormous, and pressure behind it can be immense. Instead, slowly open the plug or poke small holes in it (if it is a throwaway). A dribble is far better than a flood!

Pipes to Use in Wastewater

In the first house I built many years ago, we used cast-iron pipe. This came in lengths of about 4 feet. The problem was that in those days the sections were joined together by tapping in hemp and then filling the remaining space with molten lead. This meant you had to have a lead pot boiling all the time. As a result, over time, many plumbers suffered from lead poisoning.

Today cast-iron pipe is still used because of its strength, but compression fittings made of rubber and metal fasteners are used instead of hemp and liquid lead.

The most common piping used today is plastic. A special black plastic PVC is used for wastewater, and it comes in all common sizes.

It is easy to cut, to mount, and to glue together. Plus it weighs very little, and so working with it is actually a pleasure, compared to iron pipe.

Putting in the Potable Water System

The potable or drinking water system is completely separate from the wastewater system. It consists of pipes that bring hot and cold water to all the home's fixtures.

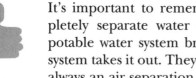

TIP

It's important to remember that there are two completely separate water systems in every home. The potable water system brings water in. The wastewater system takes it out. They are never connected. (There's always an air separation, even in sinks and tubs.)

The Water Heater

The water heater should be located in an area that is as close as possible to where you will need the water (kitchen, baths, washroom) to avoid long runs during which the heat will dissipate. Other considerations include having easy access, particularly if you're going to need to drain the tank to winterize your home. Typical spots are in the garage, washroom, or pantry. Usually the water heater is on the lowest level, so that if it springs a leak, the water will drain out without damaging the home.

TIP

If you need to put your water heater near where water damage could occur because of a leak, have a sheet metal pan built under it to capture any leaking water, with a drain that leads to the outside. It could save you

thousands of dollars in water damage, much of which
your homeowner's insurance might not cover!

Get as large a water heater as you can. I would not suggest getting
anything less than 50 gallons. In the last house I built, I put in two
50-gallon heaters, just to be sure we never ran out of hot water.

TRAP

All water heaters should have a temperature/pressure
relief valve installed, vented to the outdoors and aimed
down. These valves usually do not come with the
heater, but must be purchased separately. Their purpose is to relieve pressure in the tank if the other safety control systems fail. It is your last line of defense for
a defective heater. If the water heater should blow, it
will go off like a bomb and can literally destroy a home,
not to mention injuring or killing its inhabitants.

Heaters come equipped for a variety of energy sources. Usually
the most expensive to operate is electrical; the least expensive kind
operates on propane or natural gas. Some home heating systems
(such as Amana) make a heater that uses the same energy to heat
both water and air. This is a superefficient system that may cost you
a few bucks initially, but it will save you a bundle later on.

Installing the Potable Water System

The potable water system is logical and relatively easy to design. You
need two sets of pipes, one for hot, the other for cold. Typically they
parallel each other. Because you needn't be concerned about venting, the layout is usually straightforward. The cold water from the
inlet goes directly to the hot water heater. From there two lines, cold
and hot, spread out to all the fixtures in the house. Usually the
rough plumbing is done during framing, so you can drill through
boards to accommodate the pipes.

TIP

When drilling holes in boards to accommodate waste-water and potable water supplies, care should be taken to make sure the holes are no larger than needed to fit the pipes, and they should be spaced wide apart. Every time you make a hole in a board, you weaken the board.

Types of Pipe Used

You should use copper pipe for your potable water system, period. There are adherents who prefer galvanized pipe (a few left) and those who prefer plastic PVC. However, in my opinion, nothing does better than copper.

Here's why: Copper pipe is easy to cut and easy to assemble. Once you get the hang of soldering it, you can make perfect fittings quickly every time. Further, the copper will bend under stress without breaking or leaking when the house moves because of wind or earthquake. Finally, it is not overly expensive, and it is readily available.

TIP

To avoid "hammering," a loud noise that sometimes occurs with copper pipe, a pressure chamber should be created. It looks like a big "U" in the pipe and can be quite effective.

PVC pipe is more convenient to use than copper and considerably cheaper. Also, you only need to glue the joints together and not solder them. (Most plumbers worth their salt, once set up, can solder a joint as fast as they can glue one!)

The trouble with PVC is that it tends to crack under stress, and it is not approved for potable water in many areas of the country.

Galvanized steel pipe was used years ago. I haven't cut and used it for potable water for at least 20 years. It is the most difficult to handle, because it is heavy and lengths of pipe must be threaded. The galvanized coating is designed to keep it from rusting. However, my experience is that galvanized pipe that is more than 30 years old has a bad habit of springing rust leaks. Further, calcium deposits tend to accumulate, reducing the diameter of the pipe and volume of water flow. (It's similar to what happens when you get plaque in an artery.)

Black galvanized pipe should be used for indoor gas lines. Copper cannot be used, as it has a chemical reaction with the gas.

In rough plumbing, the pipes are brought up and terminated (usually by soldering them closed) near where fixtures will go. If you've planned well, you can come within a few inches of where you will need the water. If you haven't planned well, you may find that your fixture is actually several feet from the water supply, necessitating additional installation work.

TRAP

 When installing tubs and sinks, be sure that the potable water supply is several inches above the highest level of the sink or tub. This is to prevent siphoning and the possible contamination of the water system. If the taps were lower than the highest level, a full tub or sink could find the tap under water. A small amount of siphoning occurs when the water is turned off in such a situation, and contaminated wastewater could be sucked into the potable water system. This is something the building inspectors are usually quite careful to check for. But it won't hurt for you to be aware of and on the lookout for it yourself.

The inspection of the potable water system is usually handled by simply connecting it to the water supply and turning it on. Either it leaks or it doesn't.

Placing the Plumbing Fixtures

Because the pipes are made to fit, you can literally place them anywhere. To save in costs, however, they often are backed up to each other. In other words, the fixtures from one bathroom back up to the fixtures in an adjoining bathroom. The closer together the bathrooms, kitchen, and washroom, the shorter the pipe runs need to be.

Putting In the Electrical System

As with plumbing, the vital electrical system, though not simple, is also not that complicated. The hardest thing about it is deciding how many outlets to have on a circuit. The building code has specific requirements, so check in your area and also consult a good book on home electrical circuitry design.

Just as you have a floor plan, you should also have a wiring plan. It should specify the placement of the circuits, the size of the circuit breakers, even the gauge of the wire.

It goes without saying that any modern house should have 220-volt service. This will provide adequate power for all your needs. Usually there must be a light switch in every room that controls either a ceiling light or one wall plug. Further, all plugs must be no more than 12 feet apart (so a standard 6-foot cord will reach).

Putting In the Circuit Breaker Box

The circuit breaker box (into which the service feeds) should be at least 200 amps (the volume of electricity it can handle). Older homes used to have 100-amp boxes, but with all the modern appliances, that's usually not enough power.

Your electrical service will either come in overhead from a pole or come in underground. It will come to wherever your main circuit breaker panel will be. It's usually a good idea to locate the main circuit breaker at the rear or side so that it is not visible from the front.

To get 220 volts you will need three-wire service, two of the wires at 110 each, with the third being the ground. Each of the 110 wires and the ground wire will give you 110-volt service such as used for sockets, lighting, and so forth. Put the two 110-volt wires together, and you get 220 volts for dryers, stoves and ovens, and so forth.

TRAP

Whenever anyone does any electrical work, be sure the power is off. At a building site, you may think the power is off when it actually is on. Be sure to test every wire for power before handling it.

The circuit breaker box comes essentially empty. The wires from the electrical service (the thick multistrand ones) are usually put in by the electric company, but not always. It may be necessary to have an electrician install them. Unless you are completely familiar with electrical work, I would suggest you do not install the hot wires from the service to your box.

Someone professional will need to "populate" the circuit breaker box—that is, install the many circuit breakers you need. Populating the box is usually quite easy, since the circuit breakers just clip into place. The real trick is to know how many and what amperage. Again, a good book on home electrical circuitry can help you design what you'll need.

Once you have the circuit breaker box installed and populated, you need to run the wire from the individual circuit breakers along their circuit. Typically you'll have a single circuit that will handle, for example, all the plugs in the dining room and living room. Or, perhaps, one that will handle all the lights downstairs.

In some cases you will need a dedicated circuit (only one plug on it). This is the case for a spa (hot tub), stove, clothes dryer, dishwasher, and other appliances. Check with your local code to see what your requirements will be and with the electrician who will do the work.

TIP

It costs very little and is very worthwhile to put a dedicated circuit into whatever room you will use for your computer. This will help to avoid voltage spikes that can damage equipment.

A very important function is locating the plugs, switches, and light sockets. As noted above, the general rule is that plugs must be no more than 12 feet apart across any linear space in the home. This is so that the standard 6-foot cord on lights and other appliances can reach any plug without having to use an extension cord.

You'll also want a switch near the door of every room.

TRAP

When locating the light switches, take into account the direction the door will open. You want the switch on the opening side of the door so that it will be accessible to someone entering the room. It's poor planning to put it on the wall at the back side of the door, as someone coming in has to stumble around in the dark to find the switch.

Every room should have a wall switch that controls either the overhead light (if there is one) or at least one of the sockets. That way someone coming at night can turn on the light.

You should also have electrical sockets on the outside of the home. Four, one on every side, is what I prefer. However, it is usually acceptable to get by with only two, front and rear. They should, of course, be waterproof, and the receptacles should be GFI (ground fault interrupted).

Wiring

The building code will specify the type and minimum size of wiring that you can use. Typically it will be between 12 and 16 gauge, with 14 gauge being the most common. However, there's no reason to accept the minimum. Increase the size and you reduce the chance of lights dimming, when, for example, you turn on a hair blower.

TRAP

Be careful about increasing the amperage of a circuit breaker. You want certain sizes for different uses. For example, you want a lightweight 15-amp circuit breaker on your lights, so that it will blow at even a small short. On the other hand, you'll need a heavy 40- or 50-amp breaker for something such as an oven. Use the size specified in your wiring plan.

Use copper wire. It's not that much more expensive than the alternative, aluminum; it's much easier to work with; and you'll have fewer problems down the road. For every size of copper wire, there is a comparative size of aluminum wire. However, since aluminum is not as a good a conductor of electricity as copper, the aluminum wire will always be heavier. For example, if you're using 16-gauge copper (the smaller the gauge, the thicker the wire), you might need to use 14- or even 12-gauge aluminum for the same circuit.

Usually for all exposed installations, the wire will need to be sheathed in metal conduit. This is often the case in garages where there is no wallboard to conceal the wires. (It's not because of the appearance, but because something could cut or otherwise damage exposed wires.)

Usually for unexposed applications, you can get by with Romex, double-strand wire and ground wrapped in plastic. Some building departments, however, still insist on conduit throughout, which is more expensive, harder to string, and often more dangerous (since you can sometimes strip the insulation off the wires while running them through conduit).

TRAP

Do not run Romex inside conduit. The heat buildup could damage the wire. Run individual wires through conduit.

You will also need to run a ground (third) wire to every outlet. The ground wire must be continuous (no breaks). It must be grounded at the circuit breaker box, and the box itself must be grounded both to the ground coming to it from the service and to the cold water pipes of the home. The cold water pipes go into the ground and can dissipate electricity in that way. (Don't use the hot water pipes, because someone might disconnect the water heater and you'd suddenly have no ground.)

When stringing wire, it is common practice to drill through studs to move the wire along. If you do this, make the hole closer to one edge of the stud than the other (leave at least 2 inches of solid wood on one side of the hole). Then use a metal cover plate over the shorter side. (Figure 16-1.)

The reason for this is that the wallboard will be nailed or screwed to the studs. If the wire is close to the edge, the wallboard nails or screws could penetrate it and cause a short. By staying away from one edge, you leave enough space to avoid this problem. The metal cover plate keeps screws and nails from penetrating on the shorter side.

Also, whenever you bring a wire to an outlet, whether it be socket, plug, or switch, be sure to nail it (using a U-nail) within 6 inches of the outlet. This keeps the wire from being pulled and stretched later on when the plugs, sockets, or switches are attached. It also prevents movement in an earthquake or windstorm.

Other Wiring

In addition to electrical wiring, while the framing is open, it's a good idea to string all the other wiring that you may need. This will probably include the following:

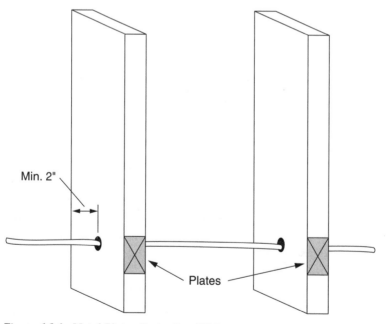

Figure 16-1. Metal Plates Protecting Wiring

EXTRA WIRING

Phone wires.   A jack in each room is a good idea.

TV cable.   Again, a jack in each room is a good idea.

Security system.   As required by the system.

Stereo speakers.   A little planning here can make a big difference later on when you move in.

Doorbells.   Be sure to wire the rear as well as the front.

Heater control.   You may want more than one; you'll want to locate the controls where no vents blow on them.

Smoke alarms.   You need one on every floor, in the master bedroom, kitchen, and elsewhere. It's a good idea to use *both* hotwired as well as battery-operated alarms.

Other systems.   As needed.

As you get all the wiring into your framing, you'll find that it begins to look like hopelessly confused strands of spaghetti. Don't despair. If you plan right, you'll discover that every wire is a different type or color. That helps you to keep them separate.

Special Considerations

When wiring a bathroom, all outlets should be a minimum of 5 feet away from a tub.

All outlets in the kitchen and bathroom should be GFI. It is far cheaper to use GFI plugs than to run a dedicated circuit with a GFI breaker all the way to the circuit breaker box. One GFI plug can service several conventional plugs on the same circuit.

TIP

Be sure that the outlet boxes are securely nailed to the wall and stick out enough so that they will be flush with the wallboard when it is nailed on. This is trickier than it seems. Don't use the markings on the boxes, as they are often incorrect. Measure the wallboard and leave that much of an overhang.

Finish Wiring

The wires are simply stuck into the outlet boxes and then folded up to get them out of the way during rough wiring. A good idea is to leave a foot of extra wire.

You will need an inspection after all the wiring is roughed in. Usually an electrical inspector who is qualified by UL (Underwriter Laboratories) will make the inspection. If there are corrections, just take them in stride. They will be for your own health and safety when living in the house.

After the wallboard is installed, it is necessary to come back and install the receptacles. This is a simple, straightforward process.

TRAP

Be sure the receptacles are installed properly. The black wire is hot; the white wire is the return. The uninsulated wire is the ground. They only go *one way* into the receptacles.

Your choice of light fixtures, switches, and plugs has grown until today it is enormous. Switches come in a variety of colors, can be soundless, can be pressure sensitive, can dim, can even be sensitive to a special sound such as the clapping of your hands.

Light fixtures vary from recessed lighting to literally thousands of lamp designs. Before making your final choice, be sure to check out your selection at a good electrical fashion store.

17
Drywall and Trim

In the old days the inside walls of homes were almost universally lath and plaster. Small sticks (the lath) were nailed across the studs, and a plasterer would then apply several coats of plaster. This produced a smooth, paintable surface that would last almost forever. However, the process was time-consuming and expensive, and when the house shifted, the plaster tended to crack and to be difficult to patch.

Plaster is still found occasionally on some expensive homes these days, but it has almost entirely been replaced by drywall (Sheetrock). Drywall is found in sheets of 4 × 8, 4 × 10, and 4 × 12 feet. It consists of gypsum plaster layered between paper. The thickness varies from a minimum of $3/8$ inch to a maximum of about $3/4$ inch. For residential usage, $1/2$ inch is the most common. However, as a firewall, usually $5/8$ inch or thicker is required.

The advantages of drywall over plaster are that it is very fast to install, it is easy to repair if it gets a hole in it, it is inexpensive, and it is far less likely to crack than plaster (although it will crack under stress).

TIP

Drywall has fire retardant properties. Because it is plaster, fire cannot easily penetrate it. Thus it is rated in the amount of time it takes for fire to get through. The thicker the sheet, the longer it will retard fire. A sheet of $5/8$- inch drywall is usually rated for around an hour. That's why it is required for use where a firewall is needed. Firewalls typically go between a garage and an attached home as well as in other areas.

Applying Drywall

Drywall is cut to fit the size of walls and ceilings. It is then nailed or screwed into place. Screwing makes for a much stronger bond and avoids the potential problem of "nail popping," in which nails pop out later on. The nails or screws are placed according to a strict schedule, typically one every 6 inches on the studs.

TRAP

While it may seem that installing drywall is a fairly simple operation, it does require skill to cut the pieces to fit. And then there's the weight. A 4 × 8 sheet can easily weigh in at 60 pounds or more. (It is, after all, plaster!) Spend a day moving these sheets around (especially when trying to put them on ceilings), and you'll find muscles hurting that you didn't even know you had!

TIP

Don't install drywall yourself. It's not that expensive to have a crew come in and do it. And they're fast. They can often do an entire house in a day or two.

Taping

After the drywall has been cut to fit, it is taped. This means that joint compound (actually, thinned plaster called "mud") is applied to all the joints, and then a layer of paper is applied on top. While it's possible to do this methodically by hand, modern tapers used high-tech machines that quickly apply both mud and paper in a single operation. Then specialized trowels on long handles quickly form them into place.

The screws or nails that hold the drywall are slightly countersunk, leaving a small depression. Mud is troweled over this to give the drywall a smooth, continuous appearance.

Exposed corners are normally covered with a thin piece of metal that's nailed in place and that provides a surface to which the mud will stick. The edge of the metal actually produces the corner, so that if something bumps into it, there's little chance of cracking.

After the drywall has been taped, it is lightly sanded to remove the rough edges, and then a finish coat is applied. This is troweled on and smoothed. Typically it extends out about 6 inches from the joint. The result is a generally smooth wall.

However, if you look at drywall that has just been taped and finished, you will still be able to detect irregularities. To make the wall completely smooth, texture is applied.

Texture is more of the mud, this time shot at the wall by a machine that puts an even surface on. There are many different varieties of finish that can be applied. Orange peel has the look and feel of the surface of an orange. A dry trowel approach gives the look of plaster. A good texture contractor can offer you many alternatives.

The Drywall Process

Here, then, are the steps to installing drywall:

STEPS TO INSTALLING DRYWALL

1. The drywall is cut to fit and then nailed or screwed in place.
2. It is taped and the nail or screw holes are covered.
3. It is lightly sanded, and then a finish coat of mud is applied to the joints, and they are again lightly sanded.
4. It is textured.
5. It is painted.

It's important to understand that usually three people (sometimes three separate contractors) are involved. The first is the one who installs the drywall itself. People who install drywall usually do nothing else.

Then there's the person who puts on the tape and finishes off the nail or screw holes. Often this is the same person who does the later texturing, but not always. There are people who do nothing but taping.

Finally, there is the texturer. This is the person (or sometimes a crew) that comes in and in a day or so does the final texturing of the drywall.

Adding Paneling

For a different look, paneling is sometimes installed. Today panel-ing has reached the stage where it is both inexpensive and amaz-ingly versatile. You can get paneling simulating almost any type of wood or other material. (An image is actually "photographed" onto plywood or compressed wood.) You can even get paneling that looks like brick, stone, or marble! Of course, if you can afford the cost, you can always use actual wood planks to final-cover the walls.

TRAP

Paneling should not take the place of drywall. Remember, drywall is rated for its fire retardancy. Paneling has a much lower rating. The paneling should go on top of the drywall.

Installing the Trim

Once the drywall has been installed, the final step is the installation of the trim. The trim is what finishes off the house. It gives it its dis-tinctive appearance. Indeed, often the difference between a house that looks luxurious and expensive and one that looks cheaply made is nothing more than the trim.

Trim is used where the walls meet the floor (baseboard), around the windows and doors (casing), occasionally where the walls meet the ceiling (crown), at waist height around a room (chair rail), as tongue-and-groove wood planks (wainscoting), and as handrails. It is available in natural wood that can be painted or as grained wood that can be stained.

TIP

These days plastic trim is widely available. It cuts quick-er, is easier to bend to fit uneven areas, and can be painted to look just like natural wood trim. However, it does not hold nails as well.

Depending on the type of finish you will have on the trim, it may be installed before or after the drywall is painted. (Drywall must always be painted.)

TRAP

Do *not* wallpaper directly onto the drywall. First use a sealer. If you wallpaper directly onto the drywall, you will not be able to get the wallpaper off later on.

If the trim is going to be painted, then generally it is put on before the drywall is painted and may be painted at the same time. However, since the drywall is usually given a flat paint coat, the trim will likewise look flat.

If the trim is to have a glossy coat or a natural wood stain, it is usually put on after the drywall has been painted.

TIP

Many types of trim come prestained or prepainted (usually only in white). These are more costly, but can save a considerable amount of time.

If you're going to used stained wood trim, then it's usually best to stain it after the entire home is finished and painted, but before the flooring is installed. Set up a couple of saw horses and lay the trim across. Stain it all at the same time so that the color matches. Then, once it's dry, cut it to fit and nail it. You can go back later to putty the nail holes and touch up areas of the stain that were bruised or chipped in the installation.

Door Trim

There are essentially four pieces of trim that go around a door. (Figure 17-1.)

1. The jamb itself, which is nailed (and shimmed) to the framing stud

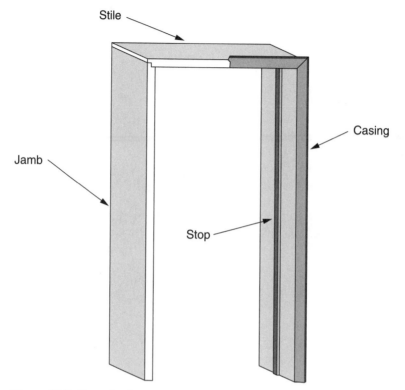

Figure 17-1. Door Jamb

2. The doorstop, which is a small stick that goes in the center of the jamb and against which the door closes

3. The casing on the inside, which finishes off the jamb and is the trim you see from the room

4. The casing on the other side

Window Trim

There are also four pieces of trim that go onto a window:

1. The window-stop, which is the trim against which the window is held in place.

2. The casing, which covers the space between the window jamb and the wall.

3. The sill, which is the bottom part of the window and which extends into the room. There may be a sill or stool trim piece on top of the sill.

4. The trim is applied to finish off the window below the sill.

If the window is aluminum or vinyl, then only those pieces that are visible within the home will be made of wood.

18

Finishing Off the Kitchen

The kitchen is the showplace of the home. It's where people gather. It's where you actually show off the quality of what you built. As a result, finishing off the kitchen is very important. You can easily spend 10 to 30 percent or more of the entire construction cost in just the kitchen alone!

That doesn't mean you must go overboard and buy a $5000 dishwasher or a $10,000 stove (although both are readily available!). It just means that the more money you are able to put into the kitchen, the better it—and your home—will look.

How Much to Spend?

There are two big considerations here. The first, obviously, is your pocketbook. You'll be limited by your budget.

The second, however, is not so obvious and tends to be overlooked by many people building their own homes. It is the norms for the neighborhood. The worst thing you can do is to overspend and create a white elephant. (A white elephant is a home that's overbuilt, so that when it comes time to sell, you can't recoup the money you put in.)

To determine what the neighborhood norms are requires a bit of detective work. You need to get into some of the homes near where you're building and see what they've done with their kitchens. Usually this isn't too difficult. Just contact an agent and ask him or her to show you any nearby homes for sale. (Almost always there will be at least a few homes.)

You don't have to fabricate a story for the agent. Simply explain why you want to see these homes. When you say that you want to make your home salable and that you will eventually sell it, the agent should be more than happy to spend a few hours showing what you need to see in the hopes of eventually getting your listing. (This is how agents develop long-term clients.)

My suggestion is that when looking at other homes, take a notebook and write down what you see. You may even want to take a camera and snap some pictures. It will make it easier later on to see what level of quality is the norm for your neighborhood

Where You'll Spend the Money

The big five areas when it comes to doing a kitchen are:

Countertops

Cabinets

Flooring

Appliances

Lighting

You'll have to divide your budget up among these.

Countertops

These days there are a great many different types of countertops available. They vary in cost quite dramatically, although all of them look very presentable.

TRAP

Be aware that certain types of countertops are in vogue, while others are not. Tile, for example, makes an excellent countertop. However, the owners of many higher-priced homes tend to favor the more expensive granite or one of the plastic tops such as Corian®. Modern laminate, which today makes a wonderful-looking countertop because colors and styles can be mixed and matched, also is less frequently seen in upscale homes because of the reminder that, in its early days, it frequently chipped and looked cheap. Of course, fashion is fickle, and what's out today could be in tomorrow.

From a building code perspective, it really doesn't make much difference what you put on the countertop. Most codes specify that the top must be nonporous and washable. In other words, food must not be able to permeate the top and rot, producing a health hazard. Therefore, a highly polished surface of almost any kind will do.

For practical purposes, however, there are four basic materials that you're likely to use. We'll consider each:

Laminate. This is a plastic-type countertop that has been popular for at least 50 years. However, don't mistake the old laminate tops you may have seen years ago with their modern cousins. Today's designs are far more colorful, the material is laid down better, the seams can barely be seen, the material is more durable, and the presentation is nothing less than awesome!

Advantages: This is probably the least expensive countertop. It's often prepared in sections at a factory, already laminated to its base and then simply assembled in the home, making it also one of the easiest to install. Alternatively, it can be glued down (the glue is similar to rubber cement) at the site. The surface is hard and easily washable, and it's difficult to chip.

TIP

If you decide to install premade laminated tops (where the laminate is already glued to the base) by yourself, be careful to get extremely accurate measurements. (You may want to have a professional do the measuring for you.) How the final product looks and how big the seams end up depends on those initial measurements.

Disadvantages: If you put a very hot pan (right out of the oven) on the surface, it could burn, leaving a permanent and unsightly brown or black mark. Also, if the installation is less than perfect, the seams will show and will accumulate unsightly dirt.

Tile. The granddaddy of countertops, tile has been used for millennia. It offers a hard surface that will not be damaged by heat. Tile is basically clay that has been molded into shape, fire-hardened, and (usually) glazed. Tile kitchen and bath countertops are beautiful and have the look of ages about them. They are more expensive than laminate, but about half the cost of the next two, Corian and granite. Tile comes in a variety of hardness (grouped 1 to 4) and is priced accordingly.

The least expensive tile is around $2 a square foot uninstalled, although the sky's the limit from there for truly exotic tiles.

Tile is available from many parts of the world. European, particularly Italian, tile has been in demand for many years. Domestic U.S. tile has improved in recent years to the point where the variety, color, and size make U.S. tiles comparable to almost anything available anywhere in the world.

TIP

For a different look, consider Mexican tiles. They tend to be irregular in shape and colorful. And they are less expensive than tile from other areas. They produce a distinctive appearance that some people like.

Installation costs vary with labor charges around the country. A good rule of thumb is to double the price of the tile itself for the cost of installation, including the installation materials needed. Smaller tiles often come attached to a threaded (fiberglass or nylon) backing, so that you can lay down a square foot at a time.

Advantages: Tile is versatile—it comes in a wide variety of shapes, sizes, patterns, and colors. It also comes in glazed or unglazed surfaces. (The glaze is the glossy surface that protects the tile.) You can choose between high gloss, semigloss, or low gloss. For kitchen and bath applications, usually a high gloss or semigloss is preferred, because it makes the tile impervious to penetration and, thus, it won't stain. Tile is permanent. If applied correctly, it can (and has) remained steadfast for centuries.

Because tile is laid down in pieces, it is relatively easy for a homeowner to install. If you get good instructions, follow them carefully, and go slowly, you can do a good job the first time out.

Disadvantages: The biggest minus with tile is that the grout tends to get dirty as the countertop is used. Although there are sealers that are helpful and cleaners that help get rid of the dirt, the grout tends to be a high-maintenance surface. Eventually, after 5 or more years, you may find the dirt is permanent, and you may want to regrout the tile to get rid of the dirt. This involves digging out the surface of the existing grout, putting new grout in, and resealing it. It's not a huge project, but it is time-consuming and messy.

Additionally, tile can crack and chip. If you slam the corner of a heavy pan or drop a dish onto it, you can do damage. On the other hand, it's relatively simple to cut out a damaged tile and replace it with a new one.

Plastic. This is a new type of surface that has been available for only a decade or so. Corian and other similar products are man-made materials. They are available in a wide variety of colors and textures, although you cannot easily create patterns with them as you might with tile or even laminate.

Plastic costs about twice as much as tile, installed. And you pretty much cannot do the installation yourself. (Indeed, in the past, before selling you the material, some manufacturers insisted that you be certified for installation from a school specializing in training people to install the product!)

Corian produces a look that defines a home as high quality. Indeed, because of the cost it is rarely found in any but upscale properties.

Advantages: There are no seams at all. A plastic surface is all of a piece from one end to the other. It comes in large slabs which, once laid, are glued together. The gluing process is so perfect that it is impossible for anyone but a professional to detect where it was done. The surface is hard and does not chip.

Disadvantages: Plastic will burn, similar to laminate, if a hot utensil is placed on it. However, the burn is easy to correct with Corian. It is cut out, and another piece is glued into place. The new surface is as good as the original, and it's impossible to detect where the burn was.

Stone. This is probably the most prestigious countertop to own at the present time. It is available as natural granite or natural marble (as opposed to synthetic marble, frequently found in bathroom countertops). It is what it says it is, stone from the ground.

It is quarried and then cut up into big pieces about $3/4$ an inch thick, which are then cut to fit for the countertop. (Stone tile cut smaller and thinner is also available.)

For years, marble was the stone of choice. However, it is porous, and as the availability of marble has diminished and its cost has gone up, granite has become popular. There is, seemingly, no end to the amount of granite available. However, granite only comes in a limited number of colors (mostly darker) and textures, depending on where it comes from. Today granite is imported to the United States from quarries around the world; hence the variety of colors and textures is growing.

TIP

If you want granite, go to the quarry or to the importer. There you'll be able to pick out the exact pieces you want and have them cut to fit. That's the only way to know exactly what color and texture you'll get.

Granite is sold by the linear inch (not the foot), based on a 2-foot-wide standard countertop size. Currently the price varies, depending on the quality of the granite, from a low of about $7 an inch to a high of about $25 an inch. That does not count the cost to have an edge cut into it, which may add several dollars per inch more. (Edges are glued-in layers to increase thickness and then cut in a wide variety of shapes.) Also, if you want a deeper piece of granite (more than 2 feet wide), the costs increase significantly. And then, of course, there's the cost of installation, which can add several more dollars per inch.

Advantages: Granite is nature's most perfect countertop. It's been created over millions of years and as a consequence has a hard, generally impervious surface, although it must be sealed. You can drop things on it, bang it, whack it and, unless there's a defect in it, not damage it.

Disadvantages: You will get a tiny seam where the different slabs of granite have been placed together. Also, if the granite should crack because it wasn't properly laid down, there's nothing you can do about it except replace it. Laying granite takes an expert, and so you won't want to be doing this yourself.

You must seal granite as soon as it is installed in order to avoid having water and other materials seep into and stain it. And you'll need to reseal it again every year or two. This is not a difficult nor complicated process and takes only a few hours. But you must remember to do it to maintain the surface.

Can I Save Money?

You can install tile or laminate yourself at a considerable savings. Numerous books are available that give you specific instructions on how to go about the installation. Corian or similar plastics usually require professional installation. I recommend that a professional handle all stone installations.

Kitchen Cabinets?

With new cabinets, the sky's the limit when it comes to price. Your costs can range anywhere from a few thousand dollars to tens of thousands, depending on the quality of the cabinets and the materials used. Add at least an additional 15 to 20 percent to have them installed.

TIP

If you've done much of the work in building your house up to this point, then you're probably qualified to install your kitchen cabinets. The only difficult part is with the trim pieces. I've always installed the kitchen cabinets in my homes, and I've been told they look good.

New cabinets are generally made to order at a shop and are delivered in sections (sometimes from across the country) to your kitchen by truck. Sometimes they are already stained or painted, and sometimes the finish painting or staining is done at the site. Although they are made to order, typically you will choose from standard sizes. If you want truly custom-made cabinets, you will usually need to contact a local cabinetmaker.

TRAP

When installing new cabinets yourself, the key is in measuring right. Measure carefully so you end up with the right type of cabinets and the correct sizes. Ready-made cabinets usually come in standard sizes, and so you can more easily place units next to each other. Be sure to abut the fronts tightly and screw them together. Any spaces or crooked alignment will show badly in the finished product.

Flooring

Many types of floors are available, including wood, tile, and vinyl. Laminate flooring (most people have heard of Pergo®) is actually a type of composite wood flooring that holds up very well. Vinyl squares are also available, and I've even seen painted cement (rarely used, but which has a definite off-beat look). Higher-priced homes may have marble, granite, or slate. These latter are the most expensive you can use, but their appearance and durability is unparalleled.

TRAP

Don't be tempted to put carpeting in the kitchen. Even a very tight weave such as indoor-outdoor carpeting won't do. The reason is that things that stain easily frequently get spilled in the kitchen. In short order your carpeting will need to be washed, and getting out all the stains can prove difficult, if not impossible.

Should I Use Vinyl (Linoleum)?

There are several advantages of vinyl over other types of flooring:

ADVANTAGES

- *Ease of installation.* Although it usually requires a professional to do a good job, it can be laid in one or two big pieces that go down quickly and produce a good-looking result.

- *Reduced cost.* Linoleum as a general rule is one of the less expensive types of kitchen flooring. However, as you move into top-quality modern linoleum, it can still be quite costly.

- *Great variety of color and design.* You get the greatest diversity of appearance with linoleum.

- *Warm to the touch and usually no-slip.* The no-slip is an important safety feature.

From the many advantages of linoleum, one might wonder how could there be any disadvantages. There are, however, several.

DISADVANTAGES

- Many linoleums have a soft surface that can easily be punctured and get tears that quickly fill with dirt and show badly. Even the hard surface type is subject to scratches or chips that become permanent and show. Dropping a knife or sharp object can scar the surface.

- It will wear out over time. The colors and patterns can fade and can even wear through. Tile, wood, or stone virtually never wears out.

- Although largely undeserved, linoleum has a checkered reputation. In years past (and to some extent still today) low-grade versions that quickly wear out were the flooring of choice in lower-priced homes. Hence, to some it has become associated with inexpensive housing. As a result, it is less frequently put into a higher-end home.

What About "Squares"?

Linoleumlike tiles made of a variety of materials are widely available in 1-square foot sizes. Because they are laid down one at a time, almost anyone can do the work and produce a good result. These, too, also come in a wide variety of colors and styles.

Squares, however, have a big disadvantage—seams. There is a seam around each square. No matter how well these tiles are laid, the seams eventually fill with dirt and show. Hence, they are seldom used in a high-quality home.

Wood Floors

Wood makes an excellent floor and has been used as such for centuries. Wood floors on many of the older homes on the East Coast are, indeed, centuries old. In Japan, wood flooring in some instances goes back three or four (or more) centuries.

ADVANTAGES

- A durable surface

- A warm look and feel

- A prestige item that always makes the kitchen and the rest of home look richer

DISADVANTAGES

- A porous surface that can absorb liquids, causing it to swell and stain. Thus, it must be properly sealed on a regular basis.

- Increasingly costly both as a material and for the labor to install it. As our forests have been cut down, there's simply less high-quality wood available, and as a result, the price has skyrocketed.

As a practical matter, wood is probably not the best choice in a kitchen, as it is susceptible to water damage. However, there are a host of new synthetics and wood substitutes available that give the look and feel of wood without its inherent problems.

Tile Floors

Tile has been the flooring of choice for thousands of years. The ancient Romans were renowned for their tile floors. It can be found in the most expensive homes in the world.

ADVANTAGES

- A hard surface that, when properly glazed, will not absorb or stain
- Difficult to damage after it has been properly laid (although individual tiles can be cracked or chipped)
- A prestige item
- Great variety in colors and sizes

As with all flooring, there are always some drawbacks.

DISADVANTAGES

- A cold-to-the-touch surface
- Can be slippery, which is dangerous in a kitchen (although there are floor tiles now that have a less slippery surface)
- Fairly costly for high-quality tiles

Stone Floors

This is probably considered the most prestigious type of flooring today. A marble or granite floor speaks eloquently of the quality of the home.

On the other hand, keep in mind that stone is the most expensive flooring, it's cold to the touch, and in some cases it can be a slippery surface. Nevertheless, if you want a kitchen floor that shouts elegance, go for stone.

Appliances

You will need most of the following appliances in your kitchen:

Stove

Oven (or stove-oven combo)

Dishwasher

Trash compactor

Instant hot water heater

Refrigerator (built-in or free-standing)

You will also need a sink, garbage disposal, faucets, and fittings.

You can expect to pay on average anywhere from a low of about $4000 for all of the above appliances to as high as you want to go. A Sub-Zero built-in refrigerator can easily cost $4000 and up. A silent Bosch dishwasher can cost $600 and more. A GE Gemini stove-oven combination weighs in at around $1200. A free-standing professional gas stove can easily cost $3000. In other words, the sky really is the limit.

My suggestion is that you check out the various home design center stores that are springing up across the country. They often contain half a dozen different model kitchens with different appliances in them. They are excellent for getting a good idea of what's available out there and how much it will cost.

Also check Chapter 2 for hints on designing your kitchen.

19
Finishing Off the Bathroom

The ancient Romans loved their baths, and we are apparently not much different. After the kitchen, the bathroom is the second most "showy" room of the house. When it comes time to sell, you can be sure that your future buyers will give the bathroom more than just a glance. The quality of the bathroom helps define the quality (and often the value) of the house.

When deciding on how to finish your bathroom, you should consider three questions:

1. What are the norms for the neighborhood?

2. How much will the way I finish the bathroom add to my enjoyment of it.

3. And, of course, what can I afford?

As long as you don't overdo it (don't upgrade beyond the norms of your neighborhood), you can justify sinking a great deal of money into your bathroom, in terms of increased value and quicker resale.

Does that mean you should spend $50,000 on a master bathroom? Probably, if it's a million dollar house; certainly not if it's a $200,000 house. The bathroom must be appropriate to the quality of the home and the norms of the neighborhood.

What About My Enjoyment?

That depends on what you want from your bathroom. If you never use a whirlpool tub, why spend thousands installing one? On the other hand, if two of you use the bathroom at the same time, be sure to put in two sinks. You'll use them.

You want to create a bathroom that's particularly suited to your needs, all the while not creating something so weird that it will make selling the home difficult if not impossible.

What Should I Use for a Countertop?

The most common countertop in bathrooms is tile, with synthetic marble running a close second. Formica used to be commonly used, but has been more rarely seen over the past two decades. Of course, for upscale homes, stone is in demand.

What About the Sink?

Use a good porcelain sink, at minimum. A stone or marble sink is even better. These can either fit into the countertop or be free-standing. Today many classic free-standing bathroom sinks give an elegant look. I know; I put one in my last home.

TIP

Be wary of metal sinks in bathrooms. They may be fine in other areas of the home, but they lack the elegance needed in this area.

What Type of Cabinets?

Cabinets are less critical in a bathroom than in a kitchen. For one thing, there are far fewer of them. The eye sees much more of the countertop, shower, and tub than the cabinets.

You may be able to get by with a premade cabinet you can pick up for a few hundred dollars. Of course, custom cabinets offer the greatest variety and the best appearance. See the last chapter on kitchen cabinets.

Should I Install a New Whirlpool Tub?

A lot depends on the following:

- Will you use it?
- Do you have the room?
- Can you afford it?

If you simply use a conventional tub-shower, you'll have a conventional bathroom. However, if you change the configuration by adding a whirlpool, you'll have a much more elegant bathroom. In a master bath, nothing looks better than a whirlpool tub.

What About the Fixtures?

You'll need to purchase and install:

Light fixtures

Faucets, outlets, and drains on tub, shower, and sink

Handle on toilet

Door handle

If you haven't purchased these before, you will probably get sticker shock when you find out the price of high-quality bathroom fixtures. For a whirlpool tub, for example, a Roman-style faucet can easily cost $500 or more. You could spend thousands on upscale fixtures for the whole bathroom.

On the other hand, you can get inexpensive fixtures for relatively little. You can get a good-quality entry-level-model sink-faucet assembly for around $100.

Just remember, however, that people who see your bathroom rarely can tell if you spent $50 or $500 on the toilet or sink. But they instantly can tell a high-quality fixture from a cheap one.

Should I Tile the Entire Bathroom?

Ceramic tile is commonly used on floors and walls of bathrooms. Alternatives consist of linoleum, asphalt or vinyl tile, or other synthetics. For a high-quality job you may want to use granite or marble. What you use should depend on the appearance you want to create, your pocketbook, and, of course, neighborhood norms.

The goal is always to get a good appearance as well as an efficient bathroom. You want to be able to enjoy it while you live there and to recoup your money when you eventually sell.

What About Toilets?

Toilets are strange creatures. We really don't want to spend a lot of time talking about them or even sitting on them, and yet they are, in reality, a focal point of most bathrooms.

A new toilet will improve any bathroom. New toilets are available in a wide variety of colors and designs. While a standard toilet can be purchased for well under $100, a modern new toilet with a striking design can easily cost $1000 or more.

TIP

For an unusual feature in a bathroom, install one of the high-tech toilet seats from Japan. These are cushioned and blow warm air and/or water! They are, however, rather pricey, starting at about $1500.

Also recheck the last chapter for more information on cabinets, countertops, and flooring.

The Aftermath

20

The Tax Man Cometh

As sure as the sun rises and sets, one day shortly after you've finished construction, you'll be paid a visit by the tax assessor. And you'll find the state congratulates you on your efforts by placing a hefty tax on them. There's no way to avoid property taxes. But you can do something about when they get raised and by how much.

Note: Tax observations are presented here to give the home builder a general overview. However, specific tax matters are beyond the scope of this book, and the reader should not rely on material presented here when making personal tax decisions. The author is not engaged in providing tax advice. If you have a tax question, you should seek assistance from a tax professional such as an accountant, an attorney, or a CPA.

Lot versus building

You'll owe property taxes from the moment you purchase your lot. However, because the lot is only a fraction of the cost of the completed home, those taxes will be fairly low. The high taxes only come about once the house is finished and a tax appraisal on the overall lot and building is made.

For example, if you pay $35,000 for your lot and the tax rate is 1.5 percent, you would owe $525 a year in property taxes. However, once your building is complete, you might find that the value of your property has jumped to $200,000. Now your taxes would increase to a whopping $3000 a year.

One way to delay the increase is to delay completing the building. Usually tax assessors won't appraise partial construction because it's too hard to judge how much is completed. They will simply charge you the valuation of the lot alone. Then, once the house is finished, they'll appraise it and charge you the combined value. If the house is delayed in completion, you continue to get charged the lot rate.

TIP

When you complete your house will have a big effect on *how soon* you'll have to pay the full property tax load.

Here's a true story. I was building my own home in a rural community in the mountains. I was paying the lot tax.

The construction took about 4 months. But as it neared completion, it slowed down. I applied for and received a temporary occupancy permit from the county, because 95 percent of the work was done. But there was a certain amount of finish work on the outside that for some reason I never got to. So I didn't file a notice of completion.

This is not to say that the tax assessor was not aware of my property. As soon as I applied for a building permit, notice of construction was sent to the county tax collector, and right as rain, an appraiser from the tax assessor's office began coming by every month.

Of course, as long as work was in an obvious state of construction, nothing was said. But once it became clear that my family was living in the house, the tax man knocked on the door.

I came outside and politely explained that although we were living in the house, it was not fully completed. When he asked if he could go inside to see, I politely said, "No." But I would let him know when the home was done.

This went on for at least 4 months, until finally on his last visit the tax man said that if I didn't let him in to see the house, he would make an appraisal on the basis of just the outside. And I would have to accept it.

I pointed out that I could challenge such an appraisal, and he pointed out that if I did, I'd have to let him inside. I consented, and he came in.

The point, however, is that I stalled for 4 months. And that was 4 months that I paid the lower lot tax rather than the higher full lot and house tax.

How Much Is It Really Worth?

There's another aspect to this story. When the tax man got inside, he looked around and took some measurements. I offered him a cup of coffee, and we sat down at the dining room table as he wrote his findings. Then I asked how much he was going to value the kitchen cabinets. He said they looked to be of high quality, so he had set a figure of $15,000. I pointed out that I had gotten a bargain on them and had paid only $6000 and that I had my receipts to prove it. (See also page 225.)

He took out his eraser and changed his figures. We continued on through every aspect of the home, including whether to count a loft as full living space or half. (We agreed on half.)

By the time he was done, we had whittled his original appraised value down by over 20 percent. And remember, the tax is paid on the appraised value.

TRAP

Property tax is "ad valorem," or according to value. Some jurisdictions are straightforward and simply take the full appraised value and apply a tax rate to it, such as 1 to 4 percent. Other jurisdictions are a bit more devious. They take the full appraised value and then cut it by, for example, three-fourths. This becomes the "assessed" value. For example, a property worth $200,000 at full appraisal is suddenly worth only $50,000 for the appraised value. Then the tax department applies the tax rate, which might be from 4 to 16 percent. The point is that the results, the amount of tax you actually pay, come out the same. The second way, however, preserves the illusion that the state is charging you tax on only a fraction of the actual value of your property. And thus you are less likely to make a challenge.

What I did was to challenge the assessor's appraisal as it was being made. The reason the assessor was so willing to go along with me is because he realized that I could make the challenge later, after the tax bill was formally presented to me. And given the fact that I had receipts for everything I bought, I might just prevail. Better to give into me now than later on, when it would come across as egg on his face.

Can you do the same thing? Possibly. Keep in mind, however, the following considerations:

1. Generally speaking, the assessor needs to see your property inside and out in order to make an appraisal.

2. In most areas you can refuse to let the tax assessor into your home. In some states, however, laws have been passed that require you let the tax assessor in for purposes of appraisal.

3. In some areas, a reassessment can be made on a partially completed home, provided a certain period of construction time has elapsed (for example, 6 months).

4. Some assessors simply aren't cooperative, may make a high appraisal, and may dare you to challenge it.

5. It doesn't pay to be unfriendly to the tax assessor. Make an enemy out of her, and you'll live to regret it.

Challenging Your Tax Bill

Once your property has been appraised, the numbers get put into the county's tax logs, and a notice is sent to you of the appraised value for the current year. (*Note:* Taxes are collected by counties or townships, even though the money or a portion of it may go to the state.)

When you receive your notice, you normally have a certain amount of time, typically 60 days, to challenge the appraisal. If it appears high, you may very well want to do this.

To make a challenge, you must follow the procedure in your area to the letter. This means filing appropriate notices before deadlines. Miss a deadline and your challenge is out until the next year.

Usually, what eventually happens is that you'll be called before a county board set up to correct any errors in evaluations, and you'll be asked to make your case. Keep in mind that these people, though probably fair, are being paid by the taxes you pay. Hence, their inclination is not likely to be to lower your taxes.

However, you may be able to make a solid case based on the following:

1. Comparable homes have been appraised for less. You'll need a list of comparables to demonstrate this and will be required to show in what ways they are the same as yours. Of course, if comparable homes are appraised similarly, then you can throw out this argument.

2. Your actual costs were less. Bring in all your receipts to make this case. Keep in mind, however, that the board might rule that whatever you paid is irrelevant—what counts is the final value. For example, yes, you paid $6000 for cabinets, but they add $15,000 of value to the property. Nevertheless, my experience has been that assessors tend to be sympathetic when actual receipts are produced.

3. There is a hardship. Some states and counties offer special dispensation (temporary) if you can demonstrate special need.

4. You previously sold a property with a much lower appraised value, and you want that value switched to the new property. In California, for example, if you're over 55 and move from one home to another (or build new) and remain in the same county, you may sometimes be able to switch the old (presumably lower) appraisal to the new property. The idea here is to keep high property taxes from swamping older and retired taxpayers.

The Deductions

Whatever your taxes end up being, the one good thing is that normally you can deduct the full amount from your federal and state personal income taxes. This can be the second biggest deduction for most people. The largest deduction is usually interest on your mortgage.

Interest on the mortgage used to buy or finance the construction of a home is usually deductible up to a limit of a million dollars. If you get a second mortgage, or the mortgage is placed on the property after the purchase or construction and is not used for additional construction, the limit is $100,000. Check with your accountant, because these limits and restrictions may have been changed by the time you read this.

When You Sell

Finally, there's the matter of tax on your property when you sell it. Currently, if you take a loss, that is, if you sell it for less than you paid, or for less than it cost you to build, you cannot take a deduction. However, if you sell it for a profit, that profit is taxable.

The question is, how much is the profit and how much of it, if any, is actually taxable. It all has to do with "basis" and selling price. The basis when you build your home is normally the cost of the lot plus the entire cost of construction. For example, if you paid $35,000 (including costs of purchase) for the lot and $150,000 to put up a house, your basis is $185,000. If a few years later you sell for $300,000 (after costs of sale), you have a capital gain of $115,000.

Sales price (after costs)	$300,000
Less basis	185,000
Gain	$115,000

Although the capital gains tax rate has been significantly reduced in recent years (and there is a strong effort afoot in Congress to eliminate it entirely), you probably still will not pay any tax. The reason is the up-to-$250,000-per-person exclusion that Congress passed back in 1997.

According to this rule, if the home is your principal residence and if you've lived in it for a minimum of 2 years, you can exclude up to $250,000 per person (up to $500,000 for a married couple) of the gain. In our example above, that means that there would be no tax to pay because the gain would be lower than the maximum allowed by the exclusion. In short, you'd be home free!

For purposes of new construction, the time limit begins the moment you get your certificate of occupancy (from the county) and move in. However, you need not live in the house continuously. The rule applies for any part of 2 out of the previous 5 years. You could live in it for a year, rent it for a couple of years, come back and live in it for another year, and still claim the exclusion.

There are also special rules if you are forced to move because of a job change or have to sell because of special circumstances such as illness. Be sure to check with a good tax specialist.

So there you have it, an overview of the taxing consequences of building your home. Overall, it's not so terrible. Yes, you will have to pay sometimes steep property taxes. On the other hand, you should be able to get a deduction for them on your federal and state income taxes. And if you make a profit when you sell, chances are you won't have to pay any tax on it at all!

21

Deciding When and If to Sell

In truth, this should be the first chapter of this book. It gives you the information you need to make good financial choices when you build your home.

However, I've found that few people will listen to what follows when they're caught up in the excitement of building their home. The reason is that they fully plan to stay there for the rest of their lives, and all of the following is predicated on the fact that you will eventually sell.

Will You Sell?

As I said, most people who build their own homes plan to stay there the rest of their lives. I know I did, every time I built a home!

Statistics, however, show that families tend to move at least once every 7 to 9 years, depending on the area of the country. What that means is that the home you're building now probably won't be the family estate forever. Rather, as time passes, changes—such as a new job in a different location, children growing up and leaving home, the birth of children, illnesses, or divorce—could mean you'll want to sell that dream home you're building (or have just completed). No, it may not seem possible now, but realistically, it's something to consider.

Build to Sell

To reiterate, this is the last thing that most home builders want to think about (unless, of course, you're putting up a spec house). However, it's a vital consideration. If you think about it beforehand, it can make an enormous difference later on. It's like the old adage than an ounce of prevention is worth a pound of cure.

But how do you know in advance what things to do that will make your property more salable way down the road. How can you determine which items you put in will add to the value and which will not? Does it make sense to put in a bigger kitchen? What about the extra cost of a laundry room? Will a sunroom add resale value? What about a deck or skylights?

When you're building, there is a sky full of options. You can't choose them all. But choosing wisely can make a big difference down the road.

The answers are tied into such things as the price range of the house, the norms of the neighborhood, as well as what kind of work you do and how well it turns out.

The Most Important Questions

When looking toward the future, it seems to me that there are at least three questions you should consider:

1. Is my home going to be modest, average, or upscale?

2. What are the neighborhood norms?

3. How big is my wallet?

Let's look at the first two questions in turn.

Is My Home Modest, Average, or Upscale?

Homes come in all price ranges. But if you divide them into three categories: modest, average, and upscale, you very quickly find that certain features are expected for each category.

For example, as noted in Chapter 18, in a modest-priced home a laminate countertop might be perfectly acceptable. In an upscale home, however, what's expected might move up to a granite countertop.

In an average-priced home, a tiled entryway might be acceptable. In a modest-priced home, however, that might be too costly to consider. And in an upscale home, anything less than a marble entryway might be considered unacceptable.

You want to determine whether your home is going to be modest, average, or upscale and build to the quality expected. Overbuild to a quality higher than the price range justifies and you won't get your money out. Underbuild and you could actually lower the value of the home!

What Is the Norm for the Neighborhood?

You don't want to build a home that's radically different from the size, style, or features of other homes in your neighborhood. You want your home to fit the neighborhood, not stand out like a sore thumb. Build a smaller, less expensive house, and you won't be able to quickly sell or get a good price. Go beyond the norms of the neighborhood, and, likewise, you're unlikely to get as much for it as you want.

Here's an example. You buy a lot in a custom area, which means all the homes are built separately, not by a single contractor as part of a tract. But all these homes have some things in common. All have at least three bedrooms, three baths, and a three-car garage and are 2500 square feet in size. If you build a home with two bedrooms, two baths, and a two-car garage that's 1500 square feet, you're going to have a problem later on. People will see your house as underbuilt. You will be able to sell, but probably not for as much as you feel it's worth.

Here's another example. You buy a lot in a modest neighborhood, mainly because the lot is cheap. Then you put up a big, expensive house. You've created a white elephant. Later on, you have a great deal of trouble getting out as much as you put in. Even if potential buyers see the value of your construction, they will shy away when faced with the lower price of comparables. They fear, justifiably, that if they buy, they will have their own troubles reselling later on.

TRAP

Beware of building a white elephant. Always consider neighborhood norms. Never underbuild or overbuild.

How do you know what the neighborhood norms are? As pointed out in various places in this book, make it a point to check your neighbors' houses. Don't rely on contractors to tell you. They simply may not know and may be guessing. Only you can tell what the neighborhood norms are.

TIP

Ask an agent to take you around. Let the agent know that when you eventually want to sell, you'll call him or her first. You won't have any problem being shown neighborhood homes.

What About Market Conditions?

Market conditions are important at the time you sell. If you sell when the real estate market is depressed, you'll have trouble recouping your money simply because there won't be many buyers out there.

On the other hand, if the market is hot when you decide to sell, you should be able to get more for your home.

TIP

Buyers usually like purchasing a custom-built home. They feel they will be getting lots of extras that the home builder put in for himself or herself. That only works, however, provided you did a good, workmanlike job of construction.

To repeat, selling into a hot market helps you recoup your investment. Selling into a depressed market makes it more difficult to get your money out. Thus, the smart thing to do is to time your sale according to the expansion periods of the real estate market.

What About a Pool, Basement, Spa, and Other Extras?

Yet another factor is your choice of amenities. Adding a basement room in California would be foolish, because buyers don't expect it and won't pay much for it. On the other hand, they would love (and will pay more for) a home with a pool or a spa.

Or what if you failed to put hardwood floors in a home in the Northeast or Northwest? These floors are considered a quality item and are valued in these areas. On the other hand, in the Southwest wall-to-wall carpeting is considered standard fare, and hardwood floors, though usually more expensive to put in, likely won't add any additional value to the property.

TIP

Here's some good advice to nail onto a post while you're building: Always keep that future buyer in mind and try to build to what he or she would like. If you build a house just to fit your own needs and desires, then it's only going to have one enthusiastic buyer—you!

You May Have to Renovate to Sell!

This can sometimes be a big shocker. Why would you need to think about renovating when you're just now building the home?

It's because by the time you sell, nearly a decade could have passed. By then, the house you finish today will certainly need painting inside and out as well as new carpeting. And the kitchen and baths you install today may be considered outdated by standards of the future.

All of which is to say that you can't really sit back and count your profits until you sell. You might end up needing to spend $10,000 to $30,000 just getting the place back into shape!

Index

About the Author

Robert Irwin, one of America's leading experts in all
areas of real estate, is the author of more than twenty
books, including McGraw-Hill's best-selling *Tips and Traps*
series. He lives in Rancho Palos Verdes, California.